Civil War
Primary Sources

Edited by David M. Haugen

LUCENT BOOKS
SAN DIEGO, CALIFORNIA

THOMSON
GALE

Detroit • New York • San Diego • San Francisco
Boston • New Haven, Conn. • Waterville, Maine
London • Munich

Titles in the American War Library series include:

World War I
Flying Aces
Leaders and Generals
Life in the Trenches
Strategic Battles
Weapons of War

World War II
Hitler and the Nazis
Kamikazes
Leaders and Generals
Life as a POW
Life of an American Soldier in
 Europe

Strategic Battles in Europe
Strategic Battles in the Pacific
The War at Home
Weapons of War

The Civil War
Leaders of the North and
 South
Life Among the Soldiers and
 Cavalry
Lincoln and the Abolition of
 Slavery
Strategic Battles
Weapons of War

Library of Congress Cataloging-in-Publication Data

American war library, Civil War: primary sources / edited by David M. Haugen.
   p. cm. — (American war library. The Civil War)
Includes bibliographical references and index.
Summary: A collection of contemporary documents that includes Henry Clay's "I Am for Staying Within the Union," Jefferson Davis's "Separation by Necessity, Not Choice," Abraham Lincoln's Emancipation Proclamation, and Robert E. Lee's farewell to his troops covers the Civil War from beginning to end.
  ISBN 1-59018-202-2 (hardback: alk. paper)
  1. United States—History—Civil War, 1861–1865—Sources—Juvenile literature. [1. United States—History—Civil War, 1861–1865—Sources.] I. Haugen, David M., 1969–II. American war library. Civil War.
  E464 .A44 2002
  973.7—dc21

2001006051

Copyright 2002 by Lucent Books,
an imprint of The Gale Group
10911 Technology Place, San Diego, California 92127

No part of this book may be reproduced or used in any other form or by any other means, electrical, mechanical, or otherwise, including, but not limited to, photocopy, recording, or any information storage and retrieval system, without prior written permission from the publisher.

Printed in the U.S.A.

★ Contents ★

Foreword 5

Chapter 1: A Nation Divided 7

Chapter 2: Opening Moves 28

Chapter 3: New Causes, Old Convictions. 47

Chapter 4: The End of the Confederacy 70

Chronology of Events 89

Index 91

Picture Credits 95

About the Editor 96

★ Foreword ★

A Nation Forged by War

The United States, like many nations, was forged and defined by war. Despite Benjamin Franklin's opinion that "There never was a good war or a bad peace," the United States owes its very existence to the War of Independence, one to which Franklin wholeheartedly subscribed. The country forged by war in 1776 was tempered and made stronger by the Civil War in the 1860s.

The Texas Revolution, the Mexican-American War, and the Spanish-American War expanded the country's borders and gave it overseas possessions. These wars made the United States a world power, but this status came with a price, as the nation became a key but reluctant player in both World War I and World War II.

Each successive war further defined the country's role on the world stage. Following World War II, U.S. foreign policy redefined itself to focus on the role of defender, not only of the freedom of its own citizens, but also of the freedom of people everywhere. During the cold war that followed World War II until the collapse of the Soviet Union, defending the world meant fighting communism. This goal, manifested in the Korean and Vietnam conflicts, proved elusive, and soured the American public on its achievability. As the United States emerged as the world's sole superpower, American foreign policy has been guided less by national interest and more on protecting international human rights. But as involvement in Somalia and Kosovo prove, this goal has been equally elusive.

As a result, the country's view of itself changed. Bolstered by victories in World Wars I and II, Americans first relished the role of protector. But, as war followed war in a seemingly endless procession, Americans began to doubt their leaders, their motives, and themselves. The Vietnam War especially caused people to question the validity of sending its young people to die in places where they were not particularly wanted and for people who did not seem especially grateful.

While the most obvious changes brought about by America's wars have been geopolitical in nature, many other aspects of society have been touched. War often does not bring about change directly, but acts instead like the catalyst in a chemical reaction, accelerating changes already in progress.

Some of these changes have been societal. The role of women in the United States had been slowly changing, but World War II put thousands into the workforce and into uniform. They might have gone back to being housewives after the war, but equality, once experienced, would not be forgotten.

Likewise, wars have accelerated technological change. The necessity for faster airplanes and a more destructive bomb led to the development of jet planes and nuclear energy. Artificial fibers developed for parachutes in the 1940s were used in the clothing of the 1950s.

Lucent Books' American War Library covers key wars in the development of the nation. Each war is covered in several volumes, to allow for more detail and context, and to provide volumes on often neglected subjects, such as the kamikazes of World War II, or weapons used in the Civil War. As with all Lucent Books, notes, annotated bibliographies, and appendixes such as glossaries give students a launching point for further research. In addition, sidebars and archival photographs enhance the text. Together, each volume in The American War Library will aid students in understanding how America's wars have shaped and changed its politics, economics, and society.

Chapter 1

A Nation Divided

Between 1820 and 1854 the U.S. government enacted several pieces of legislation to contend with the possible extension of slavery into territories destined to become future states. In 1820 Congress passed the Missouri Compromise, which allowed the Missouri territory into the Union as a slave state in return for creating the state of Maine as a place where slavery was forbidden. The measure was designed to maintain the balance of power in Congress between the representation of slaveholding states and free states. Only by ensuring the balance could citizens in both slave states and free states feel that their interests were being protected in the national government.

The Missouri Compromise was a temporary solution to a growing problem, however. The nation might be "balanced," but it was also deeply divided, and the division was geographic. Industrialized Northern states had banned slavery within their borders, while Southern states had come to rely upon slavery to run their agricultural economies. Furthermore, the abolition movement, which began in the North, was working fervently to spread its message that slavery was immoral and ruining the Union. Some Northern congressmen openly held abolitionist views, and Southerners feared abolitionist agendas might influence legislation that would put an end to the traditional way of life in the South. But just how long could the nation remain half free and half slave?

Within thirty years the people of the North and South seemed to have an answer to that question. The Compromise of 1850 allowed California into the Union as a free state in return for tougher laws to ensure that slave owners in the South could retrieve slaves who had escaped to the North. Most Southerners realized the Fugitive Slave Act would not help them hold future congressional legislation at bay. Congress was now dominated by free states, and

Southern firebrands prophesied the imminent fall of slavery and Southern culture.

In 1854 the Republican Party was formed in the North. Although not an abolitionist organization, it stood firmly against the expansion of slavery into new territories. Abraham Lincoln, a lawyer from Illinois, ran for the U.S. Senate in 1858 on the Republican ticket. Lincoln lost his race, but Republican candidates in all but two Northern states carried their election bids. To the South, this was dire news. The Senate was now dominated by Republicans. And the Democratic Party was now split between Northern and Southern factions that could not agree on a presidential candidate for the coming 1860 election.

Ironically, the young lawyer who lost his bid for senator now won his party's nomination for president. It appeared likely that a Republican president would head a Republican Senate in 1860. Southerners believed a flood of abolitionist legislation was looming on the horizon. In December 1860, after news that Abraham Lincoln had won the presidential election, South Carolina's state legislature convened a special meeting to consider its future. The legislature agreed that the federal government had become too meddlesome in and even hostile toward the right of states to manage their own affairs. Justifying its reasons in a declaration of complaints against these trespasses, South Carolina announced its decision to secede from the Union on December 20, 1860.

"I Am for Staying Within the Union"

In the decade preceding the Civil War, the divisions between North and South were obvious to nearly every citizen. Some Southern spokesmen believed the nation would have to split, since compromise with the North seemed less and less feasible as time wore on and sectional beliefs—especially over slavery—became more polarized. Senator Henry Clay of Kentucky felt a certain allegiance to his Southern brethren (Clay himself was a slave owner), but he was driven by stronger nationalist sympathies that convinced him that secession was not a solution to the nation's troubles. In this excerpt from a speech given before the Senate in January 1850, Clay makes clear his desire to maintain the Union.

I am directly opposed to any purpose of secession, of separation. I am for staying within the Union, and defying any portion of this Union to expel or drive me out of the Union. I am for staying within the Union and fighting for my rights—if necessary, with the sword—within the bounds and under the safeguard of the Union. I am for vindicating these rights; but not by being driven out of the Union rashly and unceremoniously by any portion of this confederacy. Here I am within it, and here I mean to stand and die—as far as my individual purposes or wishes can go—within it to protect myself, and to defy all power upon earth to expel me or drive me from the situation in which I am placed. Will there not be more safety in fighting within the Union than without it? . . .

Chapter 1: A Nation Divided

Henry Clay, a senator from the South, voices his desire to remain in the Union before the Senate.

I think that the Constitution of the thirteen states was made not merely for the generation which then existed but for posterity, undefined, unlimited, permanent, and perpetual; for their posterity; and for every subsequent state which might come into the Union, binding themselves by that indissoluble bond. . . . The dissolution of the Union and war are identical and inseparable; they are convertible terms.

Henry Clay, speech before the U.S. Senate, January 29, 1850.

A Hostile and Autocratic Government

The Compromise of 1850 was a volatile piece of legislation. When Senator Henry Clay proposed the measure, many Southerners were outraged that the nation would gain another free state (in which slavery was forbidden) in trade for only a tougher fugitive slave law. Southern congressmen realized that this act would upset the balance between free and slave states, giving the North a decided advantage in Congress. In response to the proposed compromise, Senator John C. Calhoun, an ardent defender of the South and slavery, made a speech in March 1850. On the Senate floor, Calhoun listed all of the wrongs that he believed the South had endured at the hands of the North, indicating that the new legislation would be another in a series of purposefully hostile acts driving the South away from the Union. In the following excerpt, Calhoun argues that the federal government is already controlled by Northern interests who have ignored Southern complaints and stripped the states of all power in order to ensure a despotic rule of the nation.

That the Government claims, and practically maintains the right to decide in the last resort, as to the extent of its powers, will scarcely be denied by any one conversant with the political history of the country. That it also claims the right to resort to force to maintain whatever power it claims, against all opposition, is equally certain. Indeed it is apparent, from what we daily hear, that this has become the prevailing and fixed opinion of a great majority of the community. Now, I ask, what limitation can possibly be placed upon the powers of a government claiming and exercising such rights? And, if none can be, how can the separate governments of the States maintain and protect the powers reserved to them by the constitution—or the people of the several States maintain those which are reserved to them,

A portrait of John C. Calhoun, a strong proponent of slavery and the Southern way of life.

and among others, the sovereign powers by which they ordained and established, not only their separate State Constitutions and Governments, but also the Constitution and Government of the United States? But, if they have no constitutional means of maintaining them against the right claimed by this Government, it necessarily follows, that they hold them at its pleasure and discretion, and that all the powers of the system are in reality concentrated in it. It also follows, that the character of the Government has been changed in consequence, from a federal republic, as it originally came from the hands of its framers, into a great national consolidated democracy. It has indeed, at present, all the characteristics of the latter, and not one of the former, although it still retains its outward form.

The result of the whole of these causes combined is—that the North has acquired a decided ascendancy over every department of this Government, and through it a control over all the powers of the system. A single section governed by the will of the numerical majority, has now, in fact, the control of the Government and the entire powers of the system. What was once a constitutional federal republic, is now converted, in reality, into one as absolute as that of the Autocrat of Russia, and as despotic in its tendency as any absolute government that ever existed.

As, then, the North has the absolute control over the Government, it is manifest, that on all questions between it and the South, where there is a diversity of interests, the interest of the latter will be sacrificed to the former, however oppressive the effects may be; as the South possesses no means by which it can resist, through the action of the Government. But if there was no question of vital importance to the South, in reference to which there was a diversity of views between the two sections, this state of things might be endured, without the hazard of destruction to the South. But such is not the fact. There is a question of vital importance to the Southern section, in reference to which the views and feelings of the two sections are as opposite and hostile as they can possibly be.

John C. Calhoun, speech before U.S. Senate, March 4, 1850.

Abolish Slavery and Save the Union

While many Southerners supported slavery (even the majority of Southerners who did not own any slaves), there were exceptions. Hinton R. Helper, a writer born in North Carolina, was perhaps one of the more prominent antislavery advocates from the South. Helper's opinion on slavery was formed entirely around his belief that the South was losing the economic race with the industrialized North. Thus, slavery was not a moral blight but an obstacle to economic growth.

In his controversial book, The Impending Crisis of the South: How to Meet It, *Helper argues that slavery has deprived blacks of income that would, by economic necessity, stimulate the Southern economy. Furthermore, and perhaps more importantly to Helper, slavery has robbed poor whites of the opportunity to find menial work in the South. In this excerpt from his book, Helper delivers an ultimatum to slaveholders to emancipate their slaves for the good of the South and the good of the Union as a whole.*

But, Sirs, knights of bludgeons, chevaliers of bowie-knives and pistols, and lords of the lash, we are unwilling to allow you to swindle the slaves out of all the rights and claims to which, as human beings, they are most sacredly entitled. Not alone for ourself as an individual, but for others also—particularly for five or six millions of Southern non-slaveholding whites, whom your iniquitous statism has debarred from almost all the mental and material comforts of life—do we speak, when we say, you *must* emancipate your slaves, and pay each and every one of them at least sixty dollars cash in hand. By doing this, you will be restoring to them their natural rights, and remunerating them at the rate of less than twenty-six cents per annum for the long and cheerless period of their servitude, from the 20th of August, 1620, when, on James River, in Virginia, they became the unhappy slaves of heartless masters. Moreover, by doing this you will be performing but a simple act of justice to the non-slaveholding whites, upon whom the institution of slavery has weighed scarcely less heavily than upon the negroes themselves. You will also be applying a saving balm to your own outraged hearts and consciences, and your children—yourselves in fact—freed from the accursed stain of slavery, will become respectable, useful, and honorable members of society.

And now, Sirs, we have thus laid down our ultimatum. What are you going to do about it? Something dreadful, as a matter of course! Perhaps you will dissolve the Union *again*. Do it, if you dare! Our motto, and we would have you to understand it, is *the abolition of slavery, and the perpetuation of the American Union*. If, by any means, you do succeed in your treasonable attempts to take the South out of the Union to-day, we will bring her back tomorrow—if she goes away with you, she will return without you.

Do not mistake the meaning of the last clause of the last sentence; we could elucidate it so thoroughly that no intelligent person could fail to comprehend it; but, for reasons which may hereafter appear, we forego the task.

Hinton Helper, *The Impending Crisis of the South: How to Meet It*, 1857.

Secession Will Not Lead to War

Neither the Compromise of 1850 nor the Kansas-Nebraska Act of 1854 (which allowed the people of Kansas and Nebraska territories to decide for themselves whether slavery would be allowed within their borders) lessened the sectional tensions between North and South. While Northern radicals argued that Southerners were out to spread slavery into new territories, the Southern firebrands contended that Northerners would stop at nothing short of the destruction of slav-

ery and the ruin of the Southern way of life. Edmund Ruffin was a Southern planter who recognized that within a decade the North would overpower the South in Congress and ultimately press its cause. He, like many, believed that the only solution was for the South to secede from the rest of the nation. In a series of articles in De Bow's Review, *a Southern journal, Ruffin maintained that separation would be good for the South, both culturally and economically. This excerpt from one of those pieces expresses his belief that secession would not necessarily lead to civil war, as many citizens feared. To Ruffin, the South could achieve its aims through peace unless provoked to action.*

The malignant hostility of feeling that is even now entertained by the Abolition Party, and perhaps by a majority of the Northern people, toward those of the South is not here overlooked or underrated. If they could, by merely willing it, they would ruin us, even while united with them under one government—and still more readily if we were separated. If the mere wish of Abolitionists could effect the destruction of our system of Negro slavery, even by the destruction of the entire white population of the South, I would fear that consummation would not be a remote event.

But *to will* and *to do* are very different things. And even Northern fanaticism (to say nothing of Northern self-interest and avarice) would be glad to forgo these gratifications if they were to be purchased only at the cost, to the North, of hundreds of millions of dollars and hundreds of thousands of lives. Even if admitting what is so arrogantly and falsely claimed by the North, that it could conquer and desolate the South, any such victory would be scarcely less ruinous to the conquerors than the conquered.

But there would be no such war and no movement toward it, because war could not subserve or advance any interest of the North. It is unnecessary to maintain the like proposition in regard to the South inasmuch as it is universally admitted. No one, of either side, has ever asserted or supposed that the South would assail or make war upon the North in consequence of their separation. Whether this peaceful disposition is ascribed to a greater sense of justice, or to the weakness, or the timidity of the Southern people, all concur in the belief that the South would desire peace and would avoid war, unless necessary for defense. Then, passing by this contingency, deemed impossible by all parties, we have only to examine the supposed inducements for offensive war and attack by the North on the South.

"But," it is urged by many among ourselves, "even if the North refrained from making war, still it would retain the direction of the federal government, and exercise its rights and remaining power—and also hold possession of the seat of government, the Army and Navy, the fortifications, and the public lands. How could the public property be divided peaceably? And, without resorting to war to enforce our right to a fair share, would not all be necessarily lost to the South?" I answer that, even if admitting all these premises, still there would be no need and no advantage for the South to seek justice through war—and no benefit to the North would be gained by withholding our just dues, either by war or in peace.

Edmund Ruffin, "Consequences of the Abolition Agitation," *De Bow's Review,* June/September/October/November, 1857.

A House Divided

When Abraham Lincoln accepted the Republican Party's nomination to run for U.S. senator in 1858, he attacked his Democratic opponent's stand

Lincoln and Stephen Douglas (behind Lincoln) debate the issue of slavery at an Illinois rally during Lincoln's campaign for the U.S. Senate.

on slavery. Stephen Douglas was a well-respected individual who advocated popular sovereignty, a belief that the people of a territory should decide on their own whether to permit slavery within their borders. Though Douglas was no friend to slavery, his advocacy of the Kansas-Nebraska Act of 1854 and opposition to measures like the Missouri Compromise, which mandated whether a state would be free or slave, gave Lincoln the opportunity to suggest that Douglas was tolerant of slavery's expansion. In his acceptance speech, Lincoln maintained that the nation must be wholly one thing or the other—either composed entirely of free states or of slave states. His "A House Divided" speech seemed to indicate to audiences that Lincoln was running on an antislavery ticket though his words only state "where we are and whither we are tending." Cleverly, Lincoln was robbing Douglas of Illinois's strong antislavery support without actually declaring an abolitionist agenda.

If we could first know where we are, and whither we are tending, we would then better judge what to do, and how to do it. We are now far into the fifth year, since a policy was initiated, with the avowed object, and confident premise, of putting an end to slavery agitation.

Under the operation of that policy, that agitation has not only not ceased, but has constantly augmented.

In my opinion, it will not cease, until a crisis shall have been reached, and passed.

"A house divided against itself cannot stand."

I believe this government cannot endure, permanently half slave and half free.

I do not expect the Union to be dissolved—I do not expect the house to fall—but I do expect it will cease to be divided.

It will become all one thing, or all the other.

Either the opponents of slavery will arrest the further spread of it, and place it where the public mind shall rest in the belief that it is in course of ultimate extinction; or its advocates will push it forward, till it shall become alike lawful in all the States, old as well as new—North as well as South.

Have we no tendency to the latter condition?

Let any one who doubts, carefully contemplate that now almost complete legal combination—piece of machinery so to speak—compounded of the Nebraska doctrine, and the Dred Scott decision. . . .

The working points of that machinery are:

First, that no negro slave, imported as such from Africa, and no descendant of such slave can ever be a citizen of any State, in the sense of that term as used in the Constitution of the United States. . . .

Secondly, that "subject to the Constitution of the United States," neither Congress nor a Territorial Legislature can exclude slavery from any United States territory. . . .

Thirdly, that whether the holding a negro in actual slavery in a free State, makes him free, as against the holder, the United States courts will not decide, but will leave to be decided by the courts of any slave State the negro may be forced into by the master. . . .

Auxiliary to all this, and working hand in hand with it, the Nebraska doctrine, or what is left of it, is to educate and mould public opinion, at least Northern public opinion, to not care whether slavery is voted down or voted up.

This shows exactly where we now are; and partially also, whither we are tending. . . .

It should not be overlooked that, by the Nebraska bill, the people of a State as well as Territory, were to be left "perfectly free" [to adopt slavery] "subject only to the Constitution."

Why mention a State? They were legislating for territories, and not for or about States. . . . Put that and that together, and we have another nice little niche, which we may, ere long, see filled with another Supreme Court decision, declaring that the Constitution of the United States does not permit a State to exclude slavery from its limits. . . .

We shall lie down pleasantly dreaming that the people of Missouri are on the verge of making their State free; and we shall awake to the reality, instead, that the Supreme Court has made Illinois a slave State.

Abraham Lincoln, acceptance speech of Republican nomination for Illinois senator, 1858.

Slaves North and South

In 1858, the same year that Abraham Lincoln argued that "A house divided against itself cannot stand," James Henry Hammond delivered a very controversial proslavery speech in the Senate. Hammond, a wealthy South Carolina slave owner, argued that every society needs two groups: one to perform all the menial labor and "the drudgery of life," and one to lead "progress, civilization, and refinement." He indicated that the South had black slaves to carry out the everyday toil while the North had working class white slaves. Although it was true that many of the North's working class fared little better than plantation slaves, Republicans seized upon Hammond's indictment as slander against the ideals of American democracy that stressed a classless society and social mobility. They pointed to the speech as further evidence that proslavery rhetoric would ruin the nation.

In all social systems there must be a class to do the menial duties, to perform the drudgery of life. That is, a class requiring but a low order of intellect and but little skill. Its requisites are vigor, docility, fidelity. Such a class you must have, or you would not have that other class which leads progress, civilization, and refinement. It constitutes the very mud-sill of society and of political government; and you might as well attempt to build a house in the air, as to build either the one or the other, except on this mud-sill. Fortunately for the South, she found a race adapted to that purpose to her hand. A race inferior to her own, but eminently qualified in temper, in vigor, in docility, in capacity to stand the climate, to answer all her purposes. We use them for our purpose, and call them slaves. We found them slaves by the common "consent of mankind," which, according to Cicero, "lex naturae est." The highest proof of what is Nature's law. We are old-fashioned at the South yet; slave is a word discarded now by "ears polite;" I will not characterize that class at the North by that term; but you have it; it is there; it is everywhere; it is eternal.

The Senator from New York said yesterday that the whole world had abolished slavery. Aye, the name, but not the thing; all the powers of the earth cannot abolish that. God only can do it when he repeals the fiat, "the poor ye always have with you;" for the man who lives by daily labor, and scarcely lives at that, and who has to put out his labor in the market, and take the best he can get for it; in short, your whole hireling class of manual laborers and "operatives," as you call them, are essentially slaves. The difference between us is, that our slaves are hired for life and well compensated; there is no starvation, no begging, no want of employment among our people, and not too much employment either. Yours are hired by the day, not cared for, and scantily compensated, which may be proved in the most painful manner, at any hour in any street in any of your large towns. Why, you meet more beggars in one day, in any single street of the city of New York, than you would meet in a lifetime in the whole South. We do not think that whites should be slaves either by law or necessity. Our slaves are black, of another and inferior race. The status in which we have placed them is an elevation. They are elevated from the condition in which God first created them, by being made our slaves. None of that race on the whole face of the globe can be compared with the slaves of the South. They are happy, content, unaspiring, and utterly incapable, from intellectual weakness, ever to give us any trouble by their aspirations. Yours are white, or your own race; you are brothers of one blood. They are your equals in natural endowment of intellect, and they feel galled by their degradation. Our slaves do not vote. We give them no political power. Yours do vote, and, being the majority, they are the depositaries of all your political power. If they knew the tremendous secret, that the ballot-box is stronger than "an army with banners," and could combine, where would you be? Your society would be reconstructed, your government overthrown, your property divided, not as they have mistakenly attempted to initiate such proceedings by meeting in parks, with arms in their hands, but by the quiet process of the ballot-box. You have been making war upon us to our very hearthstones. How would you like for us to send lecturers and agitators North, to teach these people this, to aid in combining, and to lead them?

James Henry Hammond, speech in the Senate, 1858.

The Right to Secede

Horace Greeley was an influential newspaper editor for the New York Tribune. *In the days preceding Abraham Lincoln's official assumption of the presidency, Greeley penned an editorial based on word that many Southern states were considering secession from the Union. Although many Northern politicians painted secession as treason, not everyone in the North was convinced that states did not have a right to relinquish their ties to a federal government. Greeley, an antislavery advocate, believed the Union was better off if rid of the South. Since he was not in favor of warfare, Greeley hoped—as this November 1860 editorial shows—that the government would let the Southern states peacefully exercise their right to leave an unhappy union.*

The telegraph informs us that most of the Cotton States are meditating a withdrawal from the Union, because of Lincoln's election. Very well: they have a right to meditate, and meditation is a profitable employment of leisure. We have a chronic, invincible disbelief in Disunion as a remedy for either Northern or Southern grievances. We cannot see any necessary connection between the alleged disease and this ultra-heroic remedy; still, we say, if any one sees fit to meditate Disunion, let him do so unmolested. . . . And now, if the Cotton States consider the value of the Union debatable, we maintain their perfect right to discuss it. Nay: we hold, with Jefferson, to the inalienable right of communities to alter or abolish forms of government that have become oppressive or injurious; and, if the Cotton States shall decide that they can do better out of the Union than in it, we insist on letting them go in peace. The right to secede may be a revolutionary one, but it exists nevertheless; and we do not see how one party can have a right to do what another party has a right to prevent. We must ever resist the asserted right of any State to remain in the Union, and nullify or defy the laws thereof: to withdraw from the Union is quite another matter. And, whenever a considerable section of our Union shall deliberately resolve to go out, we shall resist all coërcive measures designed to keep it in. We hope never to live in a republic, whereof one section is pinned to the residue by bayonets.

Horace Greeley, editorial, *New York Tribune*, November 9, 1860.

The Duty of the Next President

On December 3, 1860, in his fourth state of the Union address, President James Buchanan tendered some advice to Abraham Lincoln, the president elect. Everyone in America was aware of the heated divisions between North and South, and amid Southern threats of secession, the nation girded itself for some ultimatum or confrontation that would sever the two regions for good. Buchanan's presidency had failed to heal or overcome the sectional differences, and the recent election was sure to provide the needed catalyst for separation. In his address, Buchanan asserts that Southern grievances are justified, though he advocates some type of eleventh hour reconciliation. He warns the future president to act only in accordance with the Constitution and refrain from rash actions that might cause irreparable damage. Although given as cautionary advice, it is apparent that Buchanan was also defending his own actions (or lack thereof) as president amid a trying and hostile era.

In order to justify a resort to revolutionary resistance, the Federal Government must be guilty of "a deliberate, palpable and dangerous exercise" of powers not granted by the Constitution. The late Presidential election, however, has been held in strict conformity with its express provisions. How, then, can the result justify a revolution to destroy this very Constitution? Reason, justice, a regard for the Constitution, all require that we shall wait for some overt and dangerous act on the part of the President elect before resorting to such a remedy.

After all, he is no more than the chief executive officer of the Government. His province is not to make but to execute the laws. And it is a remarkable fact in our history that, notwithstanding the repeated efforts of the antislavery party, no single act has ever passed Congress, unless we may possibly except the Missouri Compromise, impairing in the slightest degree the rights of the South to their property in slaves; and it may also be observed, judging from present indications, that no probability exists of the passage of such an act by a majority of both Houses, either in the present or the next Congress.

It is alleged as one cause for immediate secession that the Southern States are denied equal rights with the other States in the common Territories. But by what authority are these denied? Not by Congress, which has never passed, and I believe never will pass, any act to exclude slavery from these Territories; and certainly not by the Supreme Court, which has solemnly decided that slaves are property, and, like all other property, their owners have a right to take them into the common Territories and hold them there under the protection of the Constitution.

So far, then, as Congress is concerned, the objection is not to anything they have already done, but to what they may do hereafter. It will surely be admitted that this apprehension of future danger is no good reason for an immediate dissolution of the Union. It is true that the Territorial legislature of Kansas, on the 23d February, 1860, passed in great haste an act over the veto of the governor declaring that slavery "is and shall be forever prohibited in this Territory." Such an act, however, plainly violating the rights of property secured by the Constitution, will surely be declared void by the judiciary whenever it shall be presented in legal form.

The most palpable violations of constitutional duty which have yet been committed consist in the act of different State legislatures to defeat the execution of the fugitive-slave law. It ought to be remembered, however, that for these acts neither Congress nor any President can justly be held responsible. Having been passed in violation of the Federal Constitution, they are therefore null and void. All the courts, both State and national, before whom the question has arisen have from the beginning declared the fugitive-slave law to be constitutional.

Here, then, a clear case is presented in which it will be the duty of the next President, as it has been my own, to act with vigor in executing this supreme law against the conflicting enactments of State legislatures. Should he fail in the performance of this high duty, he will then have manifested a disregard of the Constitution and laws, to the great injury of the people of nearly one-half of the States of the Union. But are we to presume in advance that he will thus violate his duty? This would be at war with every principle of justice and of Christian charity. Let us wait for the overt act.

James Buchanan's fourth inaugural address to the Union, December 3, 1860.

Antislavery Agitation and the End of the Union

On December 20, 1860, by a unanimous vote in the state's convention, South Carolina officially withdrew from the Union. The convention drew up a declaration that listed its grievances with the federal government. Among these were the belief that states' rights were being ignored and the recent election of a national president who had an avowed abolitionist platform. As this excerpt of the declaration illustrates, Lincoln's election, coupled with what Southerners saw as years of overt antislavery "agitation," were deemed especially "hostile to the South and destructive of its peace and safety." For such reasons, South Carolina insisted that it was compelled to dissolve the Union.

We affirm that these ends for which this government was instituted have been defeated, and the government itself has been destructive of them by the action of the nonslaveholding states. Those states have assumed the right of deciding upon the propriety of our domestic institutions; and have denied the rights of property established in fifteen of the states and recognized by the Constitution. They have denounced as sinful the institution of slavery; they have permitted the open establishment among them of societies, whose avowed object is to disturb the peace of and eloign [conceal] the property of the citizens of other states. They have encouraged and assisted thousands of our slaves to leave their homes; and, those who remain, have been incited by emissaries, books, and pictures to servile insurrection.

For twenty-five years this agitation has been steadily increasing, until it has now secured to its aid the power of the common government. Observing the *forms* of the Constitution, a sectional party has found, within that article establishing the Executive Department, the means of subverting the Constitution itself. A geographical line has been drawn across the Union, and all the states north of that line have united in the election of a man to the high office of President of the United States whose opinions and purposes are hostile to slavery. He is to be entrusted with the administration of the common government, because he has declared that "Government cannot endure permanently half slave, half free," and that the public mind must rest in the belief that slavery is in the course of ultimate extinction.

This sectional combination for the subversion of the Constitution has been aided, in some of the states, by elevating to citizenship persons who, by the supreme law of the land, are incapable of becoming citizens; and their votes have been used to inaugurate a new policy, hostile to the South and destructive of its peace and safety.

On the 4th of March next this party will take possession of the government. It has announced that the South shall be excluded from the common territory, that the judicial tribunal shall be made sectional, and that a war must be waged against slavery until it shall cease throughout the United States.

The guarantees of the Constitution will then no longer exist; the equal rights of the states will be lost. The slaveholding states will no longer have the power of self-government or self-protection, and the federal government will have become their enemy.

Sectional interest and animosity will deepen the irritation; and all hope of remedy is rendered vain by the fact that the public opinion at the North has invested a great political error with the sanctions of a more erroneous religious belief.

We, therefore, the people of South Carolina, by our delegates in convention assembled, appealing to the Supreme Judge of the world for the rectitude of our intentions, have solemnly declared that the Union heretofore existing between this state and the other states of North America is dissolved; and that the state of South Carolina has resumed her position among the nations of the world, as [a] separate and independent state, with full power to levy war, conclude peace, contract alliances, establish commerce, and to do all other acts and things which independent states may of right do.

South Carolina Declaration, December 20, 1860.

No Right to Secede

The editors of the Indianapolis Daily Journal *were initially in favor of letting South Carolina out of the Union. By allowing this, they hoped to be rid of a troublesome faction. Yet as soon as other Southern states began following South Carolina's lead, the newspaper reversed its earlier opinion. In this editorial from January 17, 1861—less than a month after South Carolina's separation—the* Journal *argues that to let any state secede when it so desires is to suggest that the Union is a meaningless and powerless sham. Furthermore, since the South has had the insolence to seize federal property (Fort Moultrie in South Carolina), the government has a duty to crush the rebellion and preserve the Union by force.*

There was a time before South Carolina had placed herself in open hostility to the Union, when we, and we believe a large majority of the North, would have consented to part with her, if she had consulted the other States, and requested permission to try a peaceful experiment as a separate nation. Her turbulence, and avowed maintenance of doctrines at war with the existence of the nation, made her, at the best, a useless member of the confederacy, and very many would have been glad to give her a chance to test the wisdom of her theories in a solitary existence. So with those States that sympathized with her, and were preparing to follow in her lead. But the case *now* is widely and fearfully changed. These States do not ask, or care to consult their associates, and learn whether it may not be possible to arrange our difficulties so as to move on in harmony as heretofore. They have put it out of our power to *consent* to anything.—They have met us, not with a request for peaceful consultation, but with war. If we concede their demands now it is the surrender of a nation *conquered* by rebel members. If we make no effort to resist the wrong we submit at once to disunion and national degradation. There is no course left, either for honor or patriotism, but to reclaim by the strong hand, if it must be so, all that the seceding States have taken, enforce the laws, and learn the traitors the wisdom of the maxim that it takes two to make a bargain.—All questions of expediency were thrust out of reach by the act which took Fort Moultrie as a hostile fortress, and hauled down the national flag as a sign of the conquest.—They have all been decided without our help. We have had no opportunity to say a word.—The seceding States have raised the issue, argued it to their own satisfaction, and decided it by war. We have been left no alternative but to resist or submit. We deplore this state of things. We had earnestly hoped that the Gulf States would give all shades of sentiment a fair opportunity of expression in the election of their Conventions, discuss their grievances calmly, request a consultation with the nation, and if they firmly and deliberately refused to abide in the Union as it is, we were willing to let them drop out, still holding our government unchanged over ourselves. In this way it *was* possible to get rid of the rebellious States, by simply diminishing, instead of dissolving the Union, which the London *Times* says is impossible. It is now, but it was not, and need not have been, if the seceding States had been willing to meet the Union fairly and come to an understanding.— Such a course would have been in accordance with the enlightenment of the age, the dictates of Christianity, and the best interests of both sections. But the hope of such an adjustment is all past, at least till the seceding States restore the government property, submit to the laws, and return to their former position of peaceful members of the Union. *There can be no conciliation with them till they do.* The government must be preserved. It is ours as well as theirs, and when they attempt to overturn it by force, we must preserve it by force. A government kicked aside at the will of any State, is nothing. The right of secession would make the government a mere accident, subsisting because thirty or forty members happened to agree in regard to it. We insist that our government is neither an accident or a trifle. It is the best yet devised by the wit of man, and is worth a dozen wars to keep. And we mean to keep it. To allow a State to rebel against it, and give way to the rebellion, is to consent to its destruction. We cannot claim that it exists even for those still remaining in it, when it is set at naught and defied by any other member. It must be whole or it cannot be at all. The people may let a member out of it, but no member can break it down to get out without breaking it to pieces. We are therefore for the most determined measures of resistance to the rebellion in the Gulf States. We insist that the Union shall be preserved till those who made it shall consent to change it. No refractory State or combination of traitors must be permitted to peril it in the pursuit of insane vengeance or impracticable theories. And if their madness leads them to open war let them suffer the doom of traitors.

Indianapolis Daily Journal editorial, January 17, 1861.

In his inaugural address as president of the newly formed Confederate States of America, Jefferson Davis asserts that seccession from the Union was forced on the South.

Separation by Necessity, Not Choice

Following the secession of his home state of Mississippi in January 1861, Jefferson Davis resigned his seat in the U.S. Congress and retired to his plantation. His retirement was short-lived, however, because on February 9 he was elected as president of the newly formed Confederate States of America. In this excerpt from his inaugural address, Davis asserts that secession was forced upon the Southern states by an unjust and hostile government. He claims the withdrawal from the Union was justified because the federal government breached some of the tenets of the Constitution, making the national contract void.

Our present political position has been achieved in a manner unprecedented in the history of nations. It illustrates the American idea that governments rest on the consent of the governed, and that it is the right of the people to alter or abolish them at will whenever they become destructive of the ends for which they were established. The declared purpose of the compact of the Union from which we have withdrawn was to "establish justice, insure domestic tranquillity, provide for the common defense, promote the general welfare, and secure the blessings of liberty to ourselves and our posterity;" and when, in the judgment of the sovereign States composing this Confederacy, it has been perverted from the purposes for which it was ordained, and ceased to answer the ends for which it was established, a peaceful appeal to the ballot-box declared that, so far as they were concerned, the Government created by that compact should cease to exist. In this they merely asserted the right which the Declaration of Independence of July 4th, 1776, defined to be inalienable. Of the time and occasion of its exercise they as sovereigns were the final judges, each for itself. The impartial and enlightened verdict of mankind will vindicate the rectitude of our conduct; and He who knows the hearts of men will judge of the sincerity with which we have labored to preserve the Government of our fathers in its spirit. . . .

We have entered upon the career of independence and it must be inflexibly pursued. Through many years of controversy with our late associates of the Northern States, we have vainly endeavored to secure tranquillity and obtain respect for the rights to which we were entitled. As a necessity, not a choice, we have resorted to the remedy of separation, and henceforth our energies must be directed to the conduct of our own affairs, and the perpetuity of the Confederacy which we have formed. If a just perception of mutual interest shall permit us peaceably to pursue our separate political career, my most earnest desire will have been fulfilled. But if this be denied to us, and the integrity of our territory and jurisdiction be assailed, it will but remain for us with firm resolve to appeal to arms and invoke the blessing of Providence on a just cause.

Jefferson Davis, inaugural address before the Confederate Congress, February 18, 1861.

Union Is Perpetual

On March 4, 1861, Abraham Lincoln was inaugurated as president of the United States. Although by then seven Southern states had seceded from the Union, Lincoln was still hopeful that they could be persuaded to return without conflict. To this end, he gave an inauguration speech which argued that states could not simply dissolve the Union at their whim. In Lincoln's view, the Union was a perpetual contract that could not be broken by its member states. Once he stated this belief, Lincoln could take necessary actions (even the use of arms) to bring the rebellious states in line under the banner of preserving the Union. This shrewdly allowed the president to skirt accusations that any aggressive federal acts would be based on a desire to rid the South once and for all of the institution of slavery.

I hold that, in contemplation of universal law and of the Constitution, the Union of these states is perpetual. Perpetuity is implied, if not expressed, in the fundamental law of all national governments. It is safe to assert that no government proper ever had a provision in its organic law for its own termination. Continue to execute all the express provisions of our national Constitution, and the Union will endure forever—it being impossible to destroy it except by some action not provided for in the instrument itself.

At his inauguration as president of the Union, Abraham Lincoln declares that states cannot simply dissolve the Union.

Again, if the United States be not a government proper, but an association of states in the nature of contract merely, can it, as a contract, be peaceably unmade by less than all the parties who made it? One party to a contract may violate it—break it, so to speak—but does it not require all to lawfully rescind it? Descending from these general principles, we find the proposition that in legal contemplation, the Union is perpetual, confirmed by the history of the Union itself.

The Union is much older than the Constitution. It was formed, in fact, by the Articles of Association in 1774. It was matured and continued by the Declaration of Independence in 1776. It was further matured, and the faith of all the then thirteen states expressly plighted and engaged, that it should be perpetual by the Articles of Confederation of 1778. And finally, in 1787, one of the declared objects for ordaining and establishing the Constitution, was *"to form a more perfect Union."*

But if destruction of the Union by one or by a part only of the states be lawfully possible, the Union is *less* perfect than before the Constitution, having lost the vital element of perpetuity.

It follows from these views that no state, upon its own mere motion, can lawfully get out of the Union—that *resolves* and *ordinances* to that effect are legally void; and that acts of violence within any state or states against the authority of the United States are insurrectionary or revolutionary, according to circumstances.

I therefore consider that, in view of the Constitution and the laws, the Union is unbroken; and to the extent of my ability, I shall take care, as the Constitution itself expressly enjoins upon me, that the laws of the Union be faithfully executed in all the states. Doing this I deem to be only a simple duty on my part; and I shall perform it, so far as practicable, unless my rightful masters, the American people, shall withhold the requisite means or in some authoritative manner direct the contrary.

Abraham Lincoln, first inaugural address, March 4, 1861.

The Border States Cannot Remain Neutral

In April 1861, the Confederates fired on the federal position at Fort Sumter in Charleston, South Carolina. Seven states had become part of the Confederacy by then and eight states along the border between North and South were contemplating whether to cast their lot with the rebels. In this May 6 editorial, an anonymous Democratic editor of the Chicago Times *points out that despite the derisive and thoughtless rhetoric of Republicans in the federal government, the border states might yet be persuaded to stay in the Union. However, in the editor's opinion, the only certainty is that these states—which will most likely bear the brunt of the conflict due to their location—cannot remain neutral for long.*

Much speculation has been indulged in as to the probable course of the Border States in the present struggle. The Republican papers, which but recently held out the idea that those States could not be kicked out of the Union, are now as thoroughly incredulous of their loyalty. They declare that their "neutrality dodge" is but a ruse to enable them to prepare for the conflict, and that in heart they are with the Secessionists. With this view, they belabor and denounce them most savagely. Their first error in estimating the disposition of the Border States was not more fatal than their present policy of abuse and villification [sic]. The true feeling of the Border States was not difficult to determine from the beginning, nor is it now to those who comprehend the character of their people, their sympathies and associations. The Gulf States were at an early day substantially a unit on the Secession question. They contained a homogenous people, with nearly an identity of sympathies and interests, and were farther off from the dangers of civil war. The Border States, on the other hand, were nearer the focus of events, and more subject to the devastations and horrors of a border war; they were far more deeply interested in the Union commercially, and far more linked with the North by ties of blood, association and business. But while this was true, it was not possible for any reflecting man to overlook the fact that the Border States were, upon the issues that lie at the foundation of the present conflict, as well as by blood and affinity, chiefly in sympathy with the people of the Gulf States. Under these conflicting feelings and interests, the Border States have taken a vasciliating [sic] and uncertain course. Their people took sides as the preponderance of interest or feeling led them. They have not, at any time approached, nor do they now, unanimity of sentiment on any course of action. Thus divided at home and liable to internal strife, they have endeavored to take a neutral position. Like all men who do not know what to do, they procrastinate and temporize, until they are forced to a decision.

Whatever may be the apology for this procrastination, there is one thing which no sane man can question; and that is, that these States cannot possibly maintain a neutral position in a war between the two sections. The attempt to do so would end in an utter failure in two months. Individuals might possibly retain a position of silence and inaction in either section, but with States it will prove entirely different. The government could not permit Kentucky, for instance, to stand as a territorial shield to the States South of her, and yet suffer her citizens to individually aid the South. Such a position might be more effective in aiding the seceders than an open revolt. It is not possible for Kentucky to control or prevent her citizens from taking such a course; nor is it possible to prevent the citizens of the North from making retaliatory aggressions upon Kentucky. However sincere the governments of the Border States might be in their attempts to maintain a neutral position, they will find it a road too hard to travel. They would be alike the object [of] suspicion and insult from both sides, and in the end would be compelled to take sides.

Daily *Chicago Times*, editorial, May 6, 1861.

★ Chapter 2 ★

Opening Moves

On April 12, 1861, Confederate gun emplacements in Charleston, South Carolina, opened fire on the federal installation of Fort Sumter in the city's harbor. The act gave President Abraham Lincoln the justification he needed to order out the U.S. militia and attempt to suppress the rebellion by force. Civil war had finally come to the nation that had been so deeply divided for decades.

Although the national conflict would drag on for five years, at the war's outset nearly everyone believed the fight would be short-lived. Northerners knew they had an industrial advantage and a larger military than the South, and therefore thought they could easily overpower the ragtag rebel army. Southerners, however, were confident that a few decisive victories on their part would show the Northern public that the war could last longer than expected, and by that, the Confederates hoped to turn popular opinion against forcing the rebel states back into the Union.

Through much of early 1861, the Confederate scheme seemed to have merit. The Confederate army had inherited many talented leaders from Northern military academies. Capable generals overcame disadvantages in manpower and supply and won several stunning victories over Union troops. The first major clash of armies at Manassas, Virginia, resulted in a rout of the federal army, and it appeared that even nearby Washington, D.C., could fall to the Confederates. To many in the North and South it seemed that the war could end quickly.

Despite the victory at Manassas, however, Southern leaders always had to contend with the larger Union army. Therefore, instead of invading the North, the Southern military chose to protect the Confederate capital of Richmond from encroaching Union troops. By besting Union generals while fighting a defensive war, the South hoped to help turn public support toward ending the war as a draw. Abraham Lincoln, however, believed it was his duty as president to save the Union at all costs. Hoping to exploit the Northern military advantages, he searched for a leader who could deliver a victory and win over the public to his cause.

In July 1861, Lincoln placed George B. McClellan in command of the newly formed Army of the Potomac. McClellan was a promising leader who had earned honors in the Mexican War. He was beloved by the men in his command because he did not needlessly sacrifice their lives. He was methodical in his approach to war, preferring to bring all his resources to bear upon an enemy before committing to battle. Lincoln hoped McClellan's popularity and military background would stir the troops to victory.

Instead, McClellan launched a painfully slow campaign against Richmond. Continually believing the enemy had superiority of numbers, McClellan patiently waited to gather all his reserves before deciding on attack. By then, Confederates would strike the Union forces a fierce blow and then move on to a different defensive line, leaving McClellan once again to gather up his troops for an assault. Frustrated with McClellan's nonaggressive tactics, Lincoln finally said at a White House war council meeting, "If General McClellan does not want to use the Army, I would like to borrow it for a time."

Eventually, Lincoln replaced McClellan, though he reinstated him briefly when McClellan's successor failed miserably. Then a string of equally ineffectual leaders assumed command of Union forces. Although no general seemed capable of garnering military laurels for the North, Lincoln still felt it his sworn mission to continue the fight. The first years of the Civil War passed, and the nation settled in to what would become a long and bloody contest of wills.

The Surrender of Fort Sumter

On April 12, 1861, Confederate artillery positions in Charleston harbor opened fire on Fort Sumter. The fort's garrison was commanded by Major Robert Anderson who refused initial terms to surrender. After thirty-four hours of shelling and many buildings afire, Anderson finally agreed to capitulate. During the siege, Charleston residents watched and wondered what this aggressive action would mean for the Confederacy and the nation. Mary Boykin Chesnut, a member of a prominent family, was one of these citizens. Her husband was an aide to the Confederate general who ordered the shelling, and the Chesnut house was therefore abuzz with the latest reports of the attack. Her diary of the war years, excerpted below, describes the day after Anderson's announcement that he would surrender.

April 15th.—I did not know that one could live such days of excitement. They called: "Come out! There is a crowd coming." A mob, indeed; but it was headed by Colonels Chesnut and Manning. The crowd was shouting and showing these two as messengers of good news whom they were escorting to Beauregard's Headquarters. Fort Sumter had surrendered! Those up on the house top shouted to us: "The

Soldiers proudly fly the Confederate flag above Fort Sumter after extensive shelling attacks forced its surrender.

Fort is on fire." That had been the story once or twice before.

When we had calmed down, Colonel Chesnut, who had taken it all quietly enough, if anything more unruffled than usual in his serenity, told us how the surrender came about.

Wigfall was with them on Morris Island when he saw the fire in the Fort, jumped in a little boat, and with his handkerchief as a white flag, rowed over to Fort Sumter. Wigfall went in through a porthole [and helped arrange the surrender of the Fort]. When Colonel Chesnut arrived shortly after, and was received by the regular entrance, Colonel Anderson told him he had need to pick his way warily, for it was all mined. As far as I can make out, the Fort surrendered to Wigfall. But it is all confusion. Our flag is flying there. Fire engines have been sent to put out the fire. Everybody tells you half of something and then rushes off to tell someone else, or to hear the last news.

In the afternoon Mrs. Preston, Mrs. Joe Heyward and I drove around the Battery. We were in an open carriage. What a changed scene! The very liveliest crowd I think I ever saw. Everybody talking at once, all glasses still turned on the grim old Fort.

[William] Russell, the English reporter for the Times, was there. They took him everywhere. One man studied up his [British novelist William Makepeace] Thackeray to converse with him on equal terms. Poor Russell was awfully bored, they say. He only wanted to see the Fort and get news that was suitable to make an interesting article. Thackeray was stale news over the water.

Mrs. Frank Hampton and I went to see the camp of the Richland troops. South Carolina College had volunteered to a boy. Professor Venable (The Mathematical) intends to raise a company from among them for the war, a permanent company. This is a grand frolic, no more—for the students at least!

Even the staid and severe-of-aspect Clingman is here. He says Virginia and North Carolina are arming to come to our rescue; for now the United States will swoop down on us. Of that we may be sure. We have burned our ships. We are obliged to go on now.

April 15, 1861, entry from Mary Boykin Chesnut's diary as it appears in *A Diary from Dixie,* edited by Ben Ames Williams. Boston: Houghton Mifflin, 1949.

"It Won't Be Such a Picnic as Some Say It Will"

As news of the firing on Fort Sumter spread across the land, families considered what the coming of war would mean to them. Some, like an Indiana farm boy named Theodore Upson, recognized that joining the Union cause would likely pit him against friends and relatives who lived in the South. Upson was too young to join the army in 1861 when he first heard that the South had seceded. Though he tried to volunteer, he was laughed away by men who were arrogant enough to think a few Northern men could whip the South in short order. Upson was probably thankful for not having to run the risk of meeting his Southern relatives in battle, but he also knew that his kinfolk in the Confederacy would fight for their cause and not surrender easily despite the boasts of his neighbors.

Father and I were husking out some corn. . . . When William Cory came across the field (he had been down after the mail) he was excited and said, "Jonathan the Rebs have fired upon and taken Fort Sumpter [*sic*]." Father got white and couldn't say a word.

William said, "The President will fix them. He has called for 75,000 men and is going to bloc[k]ade their ports, and just as soon as those fellows find out that the North means business they will get down off their high horse."

Father said little. We did not finish the crop and drove to the barn. Father left me to unload and put out the team [of horses] and went to the house. After I had finished I went in to dinner. Mother said, "What is the matter with Father?" He had gone right upstairs. I told her what we had heard. She went to him. After a while they came down. Father looked ten years older.

We sat down to the table. Grandma wanted to know what was the trouble. Father told her and she began to cry. "Oh my poor children in the South! Now they will suffer! God knows how they will suffer! I knew it would come! Jonathan I told you it would come!"

"They can come here and stay," said Father.

"No they will not do that. [The South] is their home. There they will stay. Oh to think that I should have lived to see the day when Brother should rise against Brother."

She and mother were crying and I lit out for the barn. I do hate to see women cry.

We had another meeting at the school house last night; we are raising money to take care of the families of those who enlist. A good many gave money, others subscribed. The Hulper boys have enlisted and Steve Lampman and some others. I said I would go but they laughed at me and said they wanted men not boys for this job; that it would all be over soon; that those fellows down South were big bluffers and would rather talk than fight. I am not so sure about that. I know the Hale boys would fight with [their] fists at any rate and I believe they would fight with guns too if needs be. I remember how Charlie [Hale] would get on our Dick [a horse] and ride on a galop across our south field cutting mullin heads with his wooden sword playing they were Indians or Mexicans (his father was in the Mexican War), and he looked fine. To be sure there was no danger but I feel pretty certain he could fight. May be it won't be such a picnic as some say it will. There has been a fight down in Virginia at Big Bethel. Al Beecher's Nephew was in it and wrote to his Uncle and he read the letter in his store. I could not make out which side whipped but from the papers I think the Rebels had the best of it. Mother had a letter from the Hales. Charlie and his Father are in [their] army and Dayton wanted to go but was too young. I wonder if I were in our army and they should meet me would they shoot me. I suppose they would.

Theodore Frelinghuysen Upson, *With Sherman to the Sea: The Civil War Letters, Diaries & Reminiscences of Theodore F. Upson.* Baton Rouge: Louisiana State University Press, 1943.

Lincoln Calls Out the Militia

The firing on Fort Sumter was viewed in the North as an act of war, and President Abraham Lincoln believed his constitutional duties gave him no choice but to suppress the rebellion by force of arms. On April 15, 1861, he issued the following proclamation which both called Congress into immediate session and ordered the loyal states to provide militia units for an unspecified time to retake captured federal property and put down any insurrections.

Whereas the laws of the United States have been for some time past, and now are opposed, and the execution thereof obstructed, in the States of South Carolina, Georgia, Alabama, Florida, Mississippi, Louisiana and Texas, by combinations too powerful to be suppressed by the ordinary course of judicial proceedings, or by the powers vested in the Marshals by law,

Now therefore, I, Abraham Lincoln, President of the United States, in virtue of the power in me vested by the Constitution, and the laws, have thought fit to call forth, and hereby do call forth, the militia of the several States of the Union, to the aggregate number of seventy-five thousand, in order to suppress said combinations, and to cause the laws to be duly executed. The details, for this object, will be immediately communicated to the State authorities through the War Department.

I appeal to all loyal citizens to favor, facilitate and aid this effort to maintain the honor, the integrity, and the existence of our National Union, and the perpetuity of popular government; and to redress wrongs already long enough endured.

I deem it proper to say that the first service assigned to the forces hereby called forth will probably be to re-possess the forts, places, and property which have been seized from the Union; and in every event, the utmost care will be observed, consistently with the objects aforesaid, to avoid any devastation, any destruction of, or interference with, property, or any disturbance of peaceful citizens in any part of the country.

And I hereby command the persons composing the combinations aforesaid to disperse, and retire peaceably to their respective abodes within twenty days from this date.

Deeming that the present condition of public affairs presents an extraordinary occasion, I do hereby, in virtue of the power in me vested by the Constitution, convene both Houses of Congress. Senators and Representatives are therefore summoned to assemble at their respective chambers, at 12 o'clock, noon, on Thursday, the fourth day of July, next, then and there to consider and determine, such measures, as, in their wisdom, the public safety, and interest may seem to demand.

In Witness Whereof I have hereunto set my hand, and caused the Seal of the United States to be affixed.

Abraham Lincoln, proclamation calling militia and convening Congress, April 15, 1861.

Raising the Confederate Army

In March 1861, the South realized the impending crisis and began summoning troops from the various states in the Confederacy. At first, thirteen thousand recruits were summoned, but Confederate president Jefferson Davis realized quickly that many more men would be needed to wage war against the North. In this document dated April 25, A.C. Myers, the Confederacy's adjutant and inspector general, reports on the escalation of requested numbers of troops in the days just after the firing on Fort Sumter.

Sir: In compliance with your instructions, I have the honor to submit the following report: . . . .

The recruiting service has been commenced in various sections of the country, and speedy and favorable results are anticipated. But the want of a regularly organized force for the permanent army has not been so much felt, on account of the ready response to the calls made on the several

States for volunteers. On the 9th of March, a requisition was made on the States of Georgia, Florida, Alabama, Mississippi, and Louisiana, for 8,000 volunteers. South Carolina at that time having upwards of 5,000 of her own troops in the State service, in the harbor of Charleston, was not called on for her quota. This requisition was soon filled, and the troops put in position. Again, on the 8th of April, a requisition was made for 20,000 volunteers from the several States, to be held in readiness for service. This requisition has also been filled promptly; and, finally, a further requisition on the 16th of the same month, for 34,000 volunteers, making in all upwards of 62,000 troops, independent of the 5,000 South Carolina State troops in the harbor of Charleston, above referred to. Of this whole number, including those in Charleston harbor, more than 25,000 are in position on our southern sea-board, and frontiers of Texas, leaving the remainder for operations elsewhere. Since the 16th of April, further calls have been made for 15,000 additional volunteers, and they are now being sent forward to their destination.

Reports on Raising the Confederate Army, A.C. Myers, Adjutant and Inspector General's Office, Montgomery, Alabama, April 25, 1861.

New York's 69th Regiment Leaves for War

In the weeks following the attack on Fort Sumter, both the North and South began calling for volunteer regiments to assemble for duty. Answering the call came thousands of young men flush with excitement, conviction, and the belief that the war would end quickly after a few heroic skirmishes. In New York, one such regiment, the 69th Volunteers, filled its ranks with many of the Irish immigrants who populated the city's working class boroughs. This New York Times *article illustrates the fervor of the crowds as these local boys headed off to fight the rebels.*

At an early hour the entire street was taken possession of by the regiment and its friends, and the distribution of muskets, blankets, etc., commenced. In front of Col. Corcoran's dwelling, No. 5 Prince street, a large truck, loaded with blankets, was stationed, and the recruits were required to file by this truck one by one. The rush at this point was perfectly tremendous, so eager were the men to obtain their equipments. The Captain of each company was stationed on the vehicle; and here the acceptance or rejection of the recruits occurred. . . . Passing the blanket wagon, where a blanket was thrown [to] the accepted ones, they were passed to another man, who seized their head covering and crowned them with the regimental cap.

Still another individual placed a musket in their hands, while others furnished them with a tin plate, knife, fork, and tin cup. It was not until 2 o'clock in the afternoon that all the men were equipped, after which the companies were formed, and, accompanied by the enthusiastic crowd, marched to Great Jones street, from which point the

Members of the Irish 69th Volunteers *pose in front of Union artillery.*

regiment were [*sic*] to start. For several hours there had been an assemblage of men, women and children in Broadway, mostly Irish, which had effectually driven every vehicle from that thoroughfare. Housetops and windows were crowded with enthusiastic women, who waved their handkerchiefs incessantly to the crowd beneath. Several Irish civic societies, comprising about 2,000 persons, with waving banners—the harp of Erin kissing the stars and stripes—had formed in procession in Broadway, as an escort, and patiently waited for the regiment to move.

About 3 o'clock the order to march was received, and the entire procession, civic and military, moved down Broadway. The march was a perfect triumph for the Irish citizens, vindicating their loyalty and patriotism in a most substantial manner. Col. Corcoran, who arose from a bed of sickness to accompany his regiment, was nearly killed by kindness. He occupied a carriage with one or two friends, and it became necessary for the police to protect him from the crowd which pressed upon him from all sides. . . .

If the friends of the Jeff. Davis Government ever reckoned upon any assistance from the Irish population of the North, the display of yesterday must convince them that they were mistaken. The harp of Erin floats beside the Stars and Stripes in perfect union, and will do so throughout the present struggle. If more troops are needed by the Government the Irish of this city will furnish five times the number they already have done.

New York Times, "New York's Irish 69th Regiment Leaves the City," 1861.

Rout at Bull Run

The first major land battle of the Civil War took place at Manassas Junction, a small town in Virginia, just outside the limits of Washington, D.C. There, on July 21, 1861, by a creek known as Bull Run, the Union army under General Irvin McDowell attacked the Confederates. Many local residents (including politicians from Washington) came out to picnic and watch the federal army crush the ill-trained and poorly armed Southern troops. However, the rebels proved a ca-

---

Outside of Manassas Junction at a creek known as Bull Run, Union and Confederate soldiers clash in the first major battle of the Civil War.

pable foe and their leaders turned near defeat into a stunning victory. As the Northern lines collapsed, a rout ensued. Fleeing soldiers and onlookers streamed back into the capital, causing great confusion and traffic jams along the roads into the city. In this excerpt from his report of the battle, William Russell, an English journalist, tries to move forward through the throngs of fugitives in search of General McDowell.

I had ridden between three and a half and four miles, as well as I could judge, when I was obliged to turn for the third and fourth time into the road by a considerable stream, which was spanned by a bridge, towards which I was threading my way, when my attention was attracted by loud shouts in advance, and I perceived several wagons coming from the direction of the battlefield, the drivers of which were endeavoring to force their horses past the ammunition carts going in the contrary direction near the bridge; a thick cloud of dust rose behind them, and running by the side of the wagons were a number of men in uniform whom I supposed to be the guard. My first impression was that the wagons were returning for fresh supplies of ammunition. But, every moment the crowd increased, drivers and men cried out with the most vehement gestures, "Turn back! Turn back! We are whipped." They seized the heads of the horses and swore at the opposing drivers. Emerging from the crowd a breathless man in the uniform of an officer with an empty scabbard dangling by his side, was cut off by getting between my horse and a cart for a moment. "What is the matter, sir? What is all this about?" "Why it means we are pretty badly whipped, that's the truth," he gasped, and continued.

By this time the confusion had been communicating itself through the line of wagons toward the rear, and the drivers endeavored to turn round their vehicles in the narrow road, which caused the usual amount of imprecations from the men and plunging and kicking from the horses.

The crowd from the front continually increased; the heat, the uproar, and the dust were beyond description; and these were augmented when some cavalry soldiers, flourishing their sabers and preceded by an officer, who cried out, "Make way there—make way there for the General," attempted to force a covered wagon, in which was seated a man with a bloody handkerchief round his head, through the press.

I had succeeded in getting across the bridge with great difficulty before the wagon came up, and I saw the crowd on the road was still gathering thicker and thicker. Again I asked an officer, who was on foot, with his sword under his arm, "What is all this for?" "We are whipped, sir. We are all in retreat. You are all to go back." "Can you tell me where I can find General M'Dowell?" "No! nor can any one else."

A few shells could be heard bursting not very far off, but there was nothing to account for such an extraordinary scene. A third officer, however, confirmed the report that the whole Army was in retreat, and that the Federals were beaten on all points, but there was nothing in this disorder to indicate a general rout. All these things took place in a few seconds. I got up out of the road into a cornfield, through which men were hastily walking or running, their faces streaming with perspiration, and generally without arms, and worked my way for about half a mile or so, as well as I could judge, against an increasing stream of fugitives, the ground being strewed with coats, blankets, firelocks, cooking tins, caps, belts, bayonets, asking in vain where General McDowell was.

William Russell's report of the Battle of Bull Run, July 1861.

Lost Opportunities at Bull Run

Although the Confederate army was elated at its victory at Bull Run, some of its military leaders believed the rout of Union troops should have been followed up by an immediate pursuit. If it had been, Washington might have fallen and the war might have ended more quickly. In this excerpt from his memoirs, General Edward Porter Alexander remarks on the hesitation of the army commanders to win a decisive victory that could have changed the course of history.

Quite near the field, the road crossed a small stream. Here the surgeons had established field hospitals, and about these and under shade of the trees the crowd of wounded, attendants, and stragglers was extensive. As he had ridden along the road, the President had frequently called upon men to turn back to the field, and some had done so. Here he seemed to fear that the whole army was in retreat. As he rode his horse into the stream he drew his rein, and with a pale, stern face, and in a loud, ringing voice he shouted, *"I am President Davis. Follow me back to the field!"* Not far off, Stonewall Jackson, who had been shot through the hand, but had disregarded it until victory was assured, was now having his hand dressed by Surgeon Hunter McGuire. Jackson did not catch the President's words, and McGuire repeated them to him. Jackson quickly shouted: "We have whipped them! They ran like sheep! Give me 5000 fresh men, and I will be in Washington City to-morrow morning." In that sentence, as we shall see, appears almost the only evidence of appreciation among our leaders, on that field, of the great opportunity now before them.

The enemy were routed. Jackson saw their demoralization, and felt that, if rapidly followed up, it would spread and might involve the capital itself. And every soldier should have seen in it at least a good chance to cut off and capture many thousands of fugitives retreating by long and roundabout roads.

There was little effort, worthy of the name, even to do this. Our small bodies of cavalry did their best and captured about as many prisoners as they could handle. In all 871 unwounded were taken. But to fully improve such an opportunity much more was necessary. All the troops best situated to cut the line of retreat should have been put in motion. Not only staff-officers, but generals themselves, should have followed up to inspire and urge pursuit. The motto of our army here would seem to have been, "Build a bridge of gold for a flying enemy."

Jackson's offer to take Washington City the next morning with 5000 men had been made to the President as he arrived upon the field, probably about five o'clock. It was not sunset until 7:15, and there was a nearly full moon. But the President himself and both generals spent these precious hours in riding over the field where the conflict had taken place. Doubtless it was an interesting study, the dead and badly wounded of both sides being mostly where they had fallen, but it was not war to pause at that moment to consider it. One of the generals—Beauregard, for instance—should have crossed Bull Run at Ball's Ford or Stone Bridge with all the troops in that vicinity, and should have pushed the pursuit all night. Johnston should have galloped rapidly back to Mitchell's Ford and have marched thence on Centreville with Bonham, Longstreet, and Jones, who had not been engaged. No hard fighting would have been needed. A threat upon either flank would doubtless have been sufficient; and, when once a retreat from Centreville was started, even blank volleys fired behind it would have soon converted it into a panic.

It would be vain to speculate how far the pursuit might have been pushed or what it might have accomplished had all the available force been energetically used. We were deficient in organization, discipline, and transportation, but these deficiencies are no sufficient excuse for not attempting the game of war.

E.P. Alexander, *Military Memoirs of a Confederate*. New York: Scribner's, 1907.

An Army Composed of All Classes

Foreign nations were greatly interested in the Civil War because it was a test of a new type of democracy that was largely untried outside America. European newspapers sent journalists to cover the war from both sides and report on its political as well as military dimensions. In this excerpt from an anonymous article in Blackwood's Edinburgh Magazine, *a British reporter following the Confederate army in the days just after Bull Run comments on the composition of the rebel army. While noting its multicultural makeup, he also stresses the mingling of various economic and social classes within the ranks, something unheard-of in European armies of the time.*

The *personnel* of the army is very varied. For instance, in the Louisiana regiments are seen the bronzed and fiery-eyed French creoles mingled with many Irish and native Americans from New Orleans. The Alabamans, proud of their gallant 4th, their flying artillery and other regiments, may be known by their strong frames, gay manners, and devil-may-care air. The South Carolinians, sallow in complexion, tall in stature, seldom need the Palmetto to tell the stranger the State from which they come; but in all regiments it is easy to perceive

A portrait of a rebel camp reveals the cultural and socioeconomic diversity of the Confederate army.

differences in manner and bearing, indicative of the various classes of which the army is composed.

Numbers of wealthy planters serve as privates side by side with the professional man, the shopkeeper, the clerk, the labourer; and all go through the ordinary fatigue duties incident to camp-life. We saw a poor negro servant actually shedding tears because his master, on being told off to dig a trench round a battery, would not allow him "to lend a hand."

"'Twill nebber do, massa," he said; "I go 'tarnal mad wid dem darn'd Yankees."

One day we heard a lad boasting to one of a different regiment of the number of gentlemen in his company who had thousands of dollars at their command. The latter replied, "Oh, of course they fight; but we have some in ours who have not got a cent!" The Washington artillery, comprising many batteries, is composed of the best blood in New Orleans. The gunners, dressed in light-blue uniforms, are all men of independent means. General Beauregard's son, for instance, left his father's staff, and entered as a private. The drivers are regularly enlisted into the army, and paid by the regiment; so here is a force which does not cost the country a single farthing. Their efficiency is undoubted, and the execution which they did at Bull's Run, has led to their material augmentation, and the formation of others on similar principles.

"A Month with the Rebels," *Blackwood's Edinburgh Magazine*, December 1861.

Fighting at Fair Oaks

In 1862, Union general George B. McClellan landed the federal army on the peninsula of land near the Rappahannock River in Virginia. From there he planned to move on Richmond and seize the Confederate capital. The Southerners, though outnumbered, used both ruses and stalwart fighting to slow McClellan's force. Through a series of failed moves and inconclusive battles, McClellan made little progress in his peninsula campaign. At one such battle in late June at Fair Oaks, Virginia, the Union army was struck by a Confederate attack. In a letter to his mother, federal infantryman Charles Harvey Brewster describes the deaths of many of his comrades in the fighting around Fair Oaks.

We had but 7 Companies in the fight the other 3 were on Picket. Our loss in the regiment is 27 killed, 84 wounded and 14 missing, total 125, or one out of four of the strength engaged. In Co C, we have lost in killed, wounded and missing, 21. Capt Parsons will be home before this reaches you. I did not see him from the time we went into the battle when he was wounded until just as the cars having him on board left yesterday I sent word by him to make it his first duty to tell you that I was safe. . . .

Yesterday Sunday, they had another and it is said a harder fight on our right, and tis said they piled up the Rebels like cord wood I suppose we have the Rebels cornered between Richmond and the Chickahominy and that these battles are their last desperate struggles. We are now lying behind a long line of rifle pits with an open field of 50 acres or more in front, and all the Rebels in Dixie cannot drive us from here. I have slept under a Rubber Blanket two nights by favor of the boys, and am liable to sleep without anything for some nights to come. I don't know whether Capt W is going to get well enough to take command or not but I hope he will for if there was any other officer here with our co I should go somewhere. I have been sick for three weeks and yesterday when I went into the fight it seemed as though I should not be able to stand a half an hour but I went through hard labor enough to kill a man if it were not for the excitement, but still now that it is over it seems as if I could not keep around. I was down at the hospital and saw Lieut Wetherill yesterday afternoon, and he said he should be up this morning but it is noon and he has not appeared. I cannot succeed in giving you any idea of the battle, but I know this much that I had no possible hope of coming out alive, and I thought it all over how terribly you would feel and all that, but I came out without a scratch. I look back upon it and I cannot think how it can be. It does not seem as though any man that had been there could come out unhurt.

Capt Smart of Co B (No Adams) is killed. He was killed in the last struggle last night. Capt Day of Co G (Greenfield) is killed. He was killed in the second stand we made. I presume this must seem like a very confused account but I cannot make it plainer until I can tell you by word of mouth about it. There are so many incidents crowding my head, that I cannot write clearly at all and even when I sleep, the minute I get into a doze I hear the whistling of the shells and the shouts and groans, and to sum it up in two words it is *horrible*.

Charles Harvey Brewster, letter to his mother, June 2, 1862.

Jeb Stuart Rides Around McClellan

While General McClellan's Union army was stalled outside Richmond, Confederate commander Robert E. Lee entrusted his valued cavalry leader J.E.B. ("Jeb") Stuart with the mission of reconnoitering the federal position. Instead of merely reporting on the Union right flank, Stuart rode his cavalry units entirely around McClellan's army. Stuart's dashing antics did not win Lee's heart but he was beloved by his men. John Esten Cooke, a distinguished Southern writer, accompanied Stuart on his famous ride and recalled the daring adventure in his book, Wearing of the Gray.

Such was the dangerous posture of affairs, and such was the important problem which Stuart decided in five minutes. He determined to make the complete circuit of McClellan's army; and crossing the Chickahominy below Long Bridge, reenter the Confederate lines from Charles City. If on his way he encountered cavalry he intended to fight it; if a heavy force of infantry barred his way he would elude, or cut a path through it; if driven to the wall and debarred from escape he did not mean to surrender. A few days afterward I said to him:

"That was a tight place at the river, General. If the enemy had come down on us, you would have been compelled to have surrendered."

"No," was his reply; "one other course was left."

"What was that?"

"To *die game*."

And I know that such was his intention. When a commander means to die game rather than surrender he is a dangerous adversary.

From Old Church onward it was *terra incognita* [unknown ground]. What force of the enemy barred the road was a question of the utmost interest, but adventure of some description might be safely counted on. In about twenty-four hours I, for one, expected either to be laughing with my friends within the Southern lines,

Chapter 2: Opening Moves

Jeb Stuart (right) courageously leads his cavalry around the Union flank, uniting the Confederate lines.

or dead, or captured. Which of these three results would follow, seemed largely to depend upon the "chapter of accidents." At a steady trot now, with drawn sabres and carbines ready, the cavalry, followed by the horse-artillery, which was not used during the whole expedition, approached Tunstall's Station on the York River railroad, the enemy's direct line of communication with his base of supplies at the "White House."

Everywhere the ride was crowded with incident. The scouting and flanking parties constantly picked up stragglers, and overhauled unsuspecting wagons filled with the most tempting stores. In this manner a wagon, stocked with champagne and every variety of wines, belonging to a General of the Federal army, fell a prey to the thirsty gray-backs. Still they pressed on. Every moment an attack was expected in front or rear. Colonel Will. T. Martin commanded the latter. "Tell Colonel Martin," Stuart said to me, "to have his artillery ready, and look out for an attack at any moment." I had delivered the message and was riding to the front again, when suddenly a loud cry arose of "Yankees in the rear!" Every sabre flashed, fours were formed, the men wheeled about, when all at once a stunning roar of laughter ran along the line; it was a *canard* [lie]. The column moved up again with its flanking parties well out. The men composing the latter were, many of them, from the region, and for the first time for months saw their mothers and sisters. These went quite wild at sight of their sons and brothers. They laughed and cried, and on the appearance of the long gray column instead of the familiar blue coats of the Federal cavalry, they clapped their hands and fell into ecstasies of delight. One young lady was seen to throw her arms around a brother she had not before met for a long time, bursting into alternate sobs and laughter.

John Esten Cooke, *Wearing of the Gray*, n.p., 1862.

A Coward at Fredericksburg

In late 1862, President Lincoln grew dissatisfied with Union general George B. McClellan's indecisiveness and replaced him with Ambrose Burnside. Burnside quickly staged an all-out attack

Ambrose Burnside leads Union troops in a doomed charge up the heavily fortified Marye's Heights outside Fredericksburg, Virginia.

Chapter 2: Opening Moves

against the Confederate army in Virginia. At Fredericksburg, the Southern defenders had dug strong fortifications along a hillside known as Marye's Heights. At Burnside's command, Union troops assaulted the high ground in a furious but obviously doomed charge. Robert Stiles, a major of artillery in the Army of Northern Virginia, watched from the crest of the hillside as the brave federal soldiers were cut down as they rushed directly into the Confederate's well-prepared field of fire. In this excerpt from his autobiography, Stiles tells an amusing story of his uncle, a colonel in the Confederate army, who was commanding part of the defensive line that was reached by the Union troops during the fateful charge.

We were stationed on what was afterwards known as "Lee's Hill," an elevation centrally located between the right and left flanks of our line and jutting out at quite a commanding height into and above the plain. For these reasons General Lee made it for the most part his field headquarters during the fight. Portions of the city and of Marye's Heights were not visible, at least not thoroughly so; but every other part of the field was, clear away down, or nearly down, to Hamilton's Crossing. From it we witnessed the break in our lines on the right, where the Federals came in over a piece of marshy ground, supposed to be impassable, between Lane's North Carolina and Archer's Tennessee brigade. The entire attack, from its inception to its unexpected success, was as clearly defined as a movement on a chessboard, and I confess that tears started to and even [fell] from my eyes, but a moment later a great outburst of fire a little back of the line of battle indicated that the intruders had been gallantly met by our second line, or our reserves, and in a few moments out they rushed, the victors yelling at their heels. My uncle, William Henry Stiles, colonel of the Sixtieth Georgia, and who, in the absence of the general, was in command of Lawton's brigade in the battle, told me an amusing story of this particular fight.

When his brigade, with others, was ordered to stem this irruption, drive out the intruders and re-establish—or rather, for the first time properly extend and connect—our lines, his men were double-quicking [rapidly marching] to the point of peril and he running from one end to the other of his brigade line to see that all parts were kept properly "dressed up," when he observed one of the conscripts who had lately been sent to his regiment, a large, fine-looking fellow, drop out and crouch behind a tree. My uncle, a tall, wiry, muscular man, was accustomed to carry a long, heavy sword, and having it at the time in his hand, as he passed he struck the fellow a sound whack across his shoulders with the flat of the weapon, simultaneously saying, "Up there, you coward!" To his astonishment the man dropped his musket, clasped his hands and keeled over backwards, devoutly ejaculating, "Lord, receive my spirit!"

Uncle William said the entire *dénouement* was so unexpected and grotesque, and his haste so imperative, that he scarcely knew how he managed to do it, but he did turn and deliver a violent kick upon the fellow's ribs, at the same time shouting, "Get up, sir! the Lord wouldn't receive the spirit of such an infernal coward;" whereupon, to his further amazement, the man sprang up in the most joyful fashion, fairly shouting, "Ain't I killed? The Lord be praised!" and grabbing his musket he sailed in like a hero, as he ever afterwards was. The narrator added that he firmly believed that but for the kick his conscript would have completed the thing and died in good order.

Robert Stiles, *Four Years Under Marse Robert.* New York: Neale Publishing, 1910.

The First Year of Service

Elisha Hunt Rhodes was a volunteer in the Union army. At the close of 1862, after the North's failed attempts to win a decisive battle against the Confederate army, Rhodes, like soldiers on both sides, realized the war would not end quickly. In this diary entry, written on New Year's Eve, Rhodes reflects on the past year of service and contents himself with the belief that the Union will eventually be restored.

Dec. 31/62—Well, the year 1862 is drawing to a close. As I look back I am bewildered when I think of the hundreds of miles I have tramped, the thousands of dead and wounded that I have seen, and the many strange sights that I have witnessed. I can truly thank God for his preserving care over me and the many blessings I have received. One year ago tonight I was an enlisted man and stood cap in hand asking for a furlough. Tonight I am an officer and men ask the same favor of me. It seems to me right that officers should rise from the ranks, for only such can sympathize with the private soldiers. The year has not amounted to much as far as the War is concerned, but we hope for the best and feel sure that in the end the Union will be restored. Good bye, 1862.

Diary entry of Elisha Hunt Rhodes, December 31, 1862.

★ Chapter 3 ★

New Causes, Old Convictions

After more than a year of inconclusive battles, the Union army finally achieved a marginal victory at Sharpsburg, Maryland, on September 17, 1862. President Abraham Lincoln, who had been waiting for such an opportunity, capitalized on the high spirits in the North to issue the Emancipation Proclamation on September 22. Lincoln's proclamation effectively freed all slaves within the states that were in rebellion against the Union, but would not take effect until January 1863. The announcement did not necessarily sour the good mood of Northern citizens, but it did provoke immediate controversy.

Although many Northerners supported the abolitionist cause, a large part of the populace had believed the president when he had declared at the outset that the war would be fought strictly to save the Union. Saving the nation was a valiant cause; freeing slaves seemed a less worthwhile aim to men risking their lives in battle. Racism was still deeply entrenched in the North, and the Emancipation Proclamation only enflamed long-standing prejudices.

Part of the proclamation allowed for black men to join the military ranks, and an act of Congress followed suit that legally permitted blacks to fight as combat soldiers. Many whites both in and out of uniform felt the law was intolerable. To them, this was a white man's war; allowing African Americans into the ranks only emphasized, through twisted logic, that overcoming slavery was now part of the national agenda. Undaunted by the racist attitudes, black men by the thousands volunteered for duty, but were forced to serve in segregated units. Still, these recruits performed bravely, gathering the praise of many white officers who witnessed their courage.

The Emancipation Proclamation may have brought mixed feelings at home, but it provoked the anticipated response from European nations. Since the war's beginning, the Confederacy had been trying to enlist the aid of Britain and

France. Because these nations prized Southern cotton and had no love for the "democratic experiment" that was America, the European governments did supply arms and materiel to the Confederate cause. But when Lincoln issued his proclamation, European nations curtailed much of their aid. Their enlightened governments had banned slavery in decades past, and they feared appearing hypocritical in the eyes of the world if they openly supported a proslavery government.

Of course, the lost hope of gaining valuable allies wounded the South, but Confederate leaders downplayed Lincoln's decree. Propagandists logically noted that the Emancipation had no real impact since most Southern states were beyond the reach of federal authority. It was one thing to announce that slaves were free, but quite another thing to effect their freedom. Confederate officials also noted that the Emancipation Proclamation was a wartime measure. It was not a law enacted by Congress, and therefore there was hope—however faint—that Congress could declare it unconstitutional. But perhaps most beneficially, the proclamation made plain what secessionists had stated for years: The federal government was determined to wage war on slavery. This steeled Southerners—even those who did not hold slaves—to continue the fight against the potential destruction of the Southern way of life.

A Southern Seamstress' Song

When the Civil War began, bands of patriotic Southern women gathered to sew uniforms or quilt blankets for the soldiers. The earliest ventures were often characterized by more enthusiasm than skill as many of the sewn garments fell apart from poor stitching. By the middle years of the war, however, Southern women's sewing circles had improved their efforts and turned out rugged gear to stand up to the harsh elements. This 1862 song sung by seamstresses reminds the women to hone their skills for the war effort and to recognize that their tailored clothes and blankets are helping their beloved husbands and sons continue the fight for Southern independence.

Stitch, stitch, stitch,
Little needle swiftly fly,
Brightly glittering as you go;
Every time that you pass by
Warm's my heart with pity's glow.
Dreams of comfort that will cheer,
Through winter's cold the volunteer,
Dreams of courage you will bring,
Smile on me like flowers in spring.

Stitch, stitch, stitch,
Swiftly little needle fly,
Through this flannel soft and warm;
Though with cold the soldier sigh,
This will sure keep out the storm.
Set the buttons close and tight,
Out to shut the winter's damp;
There'll be none to fix them right.
In the soldier's tented camp.

Stitch, stitch, stitch;
Ah! needle, do not linger;
Close the thread, make firm the knot;
There'll be no dainty finger
To arrange a seam forgot.
Though small and tiny you may be,
Do all you are able;
A lion once a mouse set free,
As says the pretty fable.

Stitch, stitch, stitch,
Swiftly little needle glide,
Thine's a pleasant labor;
To clothe the soldier be thy pride,
While he wields the sabre.
Ours are tireless hearts and hands;
To Southern wives and mothers,
All who join our warlike bands
Are our friends and brothers.

Stitch, stitch, stitch,
Little needle swiftly fly,
From the morning until eve,
As the moments pass thee by,
These substantial comforts weave.
Busy thoughts are at our hearts—
Thoughts of hopeful cheer,
As we toil till day departs
For the noble volunteer.

Quick, quick, quick,
Swifter little needle go;
From our home's most pleasant fires
Let a loving greeting flow
To our brothers and our sires.
We have tears for those who fall,
Smiles for those who laugh at fear—
Hope and sympathy for all,
Every noble volunteer.

Unknown, "A Southern Woman's Song," 1862.

In a reenactment of the Civil War South, a woman sews a quilt destined for a shipment of supplies for Confederate soldiers.

A Woman's Mission

Sarah Morgan was the daughter of a Louisiana judge. She lived in New Orleans when it was held by General Benjamin Butler's Union army of occupation. Morgan kept a diary of her life and recorded what she believed was the futile efforts of a proud Southern people to resist the superior forces and weapons of the North. Although she believes herself to be a patriot of her state, she scorns the vulgar acts of other female residents who spit at Northern troops and even go so far as to refuse giving aid and comfort to their sick and injured. Morgan believes that as a proper, chivalrous daughter of the South, it is her duty to carry out a woman's mission of tending to any person in need and to refrain from getting involved in the evils of politics. In this June 1862 diary entry, Morgan makes plain her attitude toward the disgraceful women of New Orleans and reveals how helpless she feels in not being able to do more for a sick Union officer named Biddle and others like him who share in the atrocities of the war.

To day I believe I am tired of life. I am weary of every thing. I wish I could find some "lodge in some vast wilderness" where I could be in peace and quiet; where I would never hear of war, or rumors of war, of lying, slandering, and all uncharitableness; where I could eat my bread in thanksgiving and trust God alone in all things; a place where I would never hear a woman talk politics or lay down the law—Bah! how it disgusts me! What paradise that would be, if such a place is to be found on earth! I am afraid it is not. What a consolation it is to remember there are no "Politics" in heaven! I reserve to myself the privilege of writing my opinions, since I trouble no one with the expression of them; the disgust I have experienced from listening to others, I hope will forever prevent me from becoming a "Patriotic woman." In my opinion, the Southern women, and some few of the men, have disgraced themselves by their rude, ill mannered behavior in many instances. I insist, that if the valor and chivalry of our men cannot save our country, I would rather have it conquered by a brave race, than owe its liberty to the Billingsgate [pretentious] oratory and demonstrations of some of these "ladies." If the women have the upper hand then, as they have now, I would not like to live in a country governed by such tongues.

Do I consider the female who could spit in a gentleman's face merely because he wore United States buttons, as a fit associate for me? Lieut. Biddle assured me he did not pass a street in New Orleans without being most grossly insulted by *ladies*. It was a friend of his into whose face a lady *spit* as he walked quietly by without looking at her. (Wonder if she did it to attract his attention?) He had the sense to apply to her husband and give him two minutes to apologize or die, and of course he chose the former. Such things are enough to disgust anyone. "Loud" women, what a contempt I have for you! How I despise your vulgarity!

Some of these Ultra Secessionists evidently very recently from "down East" who think themselves obliged to "kick up their heels over the Bonny blue flag" as Brother describes female patriotism, shriek out "What! see those vile Northerners pass patiently? No true Southerner could see it without rage! I could kill them! I hate them with all my soul, the murderers, liars, thieves, rascals! You are no Southerner if you do not hate them as much as I!" Ah ça! a true blue Yankee tell me that I, born and bred here, am no Southerner! I always think "It is well for you, my friend, to save your credit, else you might be suspected by some people, though your violence is enough for me." I always say "*You* may do as you please; my brothers are fighting for me, and doing their duty, so this excess of patriotism is unnecessary for me as my position is too well known to make any demonstrations requisite." I flatter myself that "tells."

This war has brought out wicked, malignant feelings that I did not believe could dwell in woman's heart. I see some with the holiest eyes, so holy one would think the very spirit of Charity lived in them and all Christian meekness, go off in a mad tirade of abuse and say with the holy eyes wonderously changed "I hope God will send down plague, Yellow fever, famine, on these vile Yankees, and that not one will escape death." O what unutterable horror that remark causes me as often as I hear it! I think of the many mothers, wives and sisters who wait as anxiously, pray as fervently in their faraway lonesome homes for their dear ones, as we do here; I fancy them waiting day after day for the footsteps that will never come, growing more sad, lonely, and heartbroken as the days wear on; I think of how awful it would be to me if one would say "your brothers are dead," how it would crush all life and happiness out of me; and I say "God forgive these poor women! They know not what they say!" O woman! into what loathsome violence you have debased your holy mission! God will punish us for our hardheartedness.

Not a square off, in the new theater, lie more than a hundred sick soldiers. What woman has stretched out her hand to save them, to give them a cup of cold water? Where is the charity which should ignore nations and creeds, and administer help to the Indian or Heathen indifferently? Gone! all gone in Union versus Secession! *That* is what the American War has brought us. If I was independent, if I could work my own will without causing others to suffer for my deeds, I would not be poring over this stupid page, I would not be idly reading or sewing. I would put aside woman's trash, take up Woman's duty, and I would stand by some forsaken man and bid him God speed as he closes his dying eyes. *That* is Woman's mission! and not Preaching and Politics. I say I would, yet here I sit! O for liberty! the liberty that *dares* do what conscience dictates, and scorns all smaller rules!

If I could help these dying men! Yet it is as impossible as though I was a chained bear. I cant put out my hand. I am threatened with Coventry [ostracism] because I sent a custard to a sick man who is in the army, and with the anathema of society because I said if

I could possibly do anything for Mr Biddle—at a distance—(he is sick) I would like to very much. . . . I would like to see the *man* who *dared* harm my father's daughter! But as he seems to think our conduct reflects on him, there is no alternative. Die, poor men, without a woman's hand to close your eyes! We women are too *patriotic* to help you! I look eagerly on, cry in my soul "I wish—"; you die, God judges me. Behold the woman who dares not risk private ties for God's glory and her professed religion! Coward, helpless woman that I am! If I was free!

Sarah Morgan, *The Civil War Diary of Sarah Morgan*. Athens: University of Georgia Press, 1991.

Government Meddling Is Prolonging the War

Robert Gould Shaw was the commander of the 54th Massachusetts Regiment, the most prominent black unit that served in the Civil War. In a letter to his mother dated July 23, 1862, Shaw shows his frustration at what he sees as the unnecessary prolonging of the war by the interference of the government in the training and discipline of Northern troops. Shaw's beliefs were shared by many Union officers who assumed that the North had not achieved any victories in the first year of combat precisely because of government meddling in the affairs of the army.

Dear Mother,

As I mentioned in a short note to Father day before yesterday, I have received several letters from home since we arrived here. Yesterday I got his of 18th July. I was very sorry to hear you had not been well. I hope you are careful about exposing yourself.

Now Congress has adjourned, perhaps the war will be more vigorously and systematically carried on, though I think we should do better still, if the President and his Cabinet would adjourn too. Our republican government never managed the country with a very firm hand, even in time of peace, and one year of war has shown pretty clearly that that is not its forte. We may finish the war, but it will certainly be with a much greater loss of time, life, and money than if we had had some men, any man almost, with a few common-sense military ideas, to manage matters, without being meddled with and badgered by a lot of men who show the greatest ignorance about the commonest things. Who but a crazy man could have stopped the enlisting, because there were 700,000 men mustered into the service? Taking out of these the sick, the deserters, and those on detached service in hospitals, barracks, &c., we couldn't have more than 500,000 before the campaign began. All these were scattered about the country, and we had no reserve, or recruiting stations to draw from. . . .

I see that the papers are all crying out and wondering because there are at least forty thousand men absent and unaccounted for, who should be with McClellan, or this army. What is the reason they can go off with impunity and be out of the way, just when they are wanted? Because when it was necessary to shoot some men last winter for desertion, the President pardoned them, and every one thought it was too bad to punish our "brave Volunteers" for just going home to see their families for a little while, without permission. They know now that nothing will be done to them, and many of them are deserting to enlist in the new regiments for $100 bounty [cash payment made for enlisting, set by the U.S. Congress in July, 1861]. The same policy has been followed with the army all along.

Senator Wilson [Henry Wilson of Massachusetts] makes a great fuss because some of his constituents are court-martialed and condemned to the Washington Penitentiary, for what he calls "trifling offences." One "trifling offence" is leaving the ranks on the march. The regiment goes into a fight after four hours marching, and only two thirds or one half of the men are present. This may seem a "trifling offence" to some men, but it certainly is not. Men mustn't be severely punished for disobeying orders, for deserting, for insulting and even striking their officers and non-commissioned officers, and the result is that they do just about what they please. If the majority of them hadn't more intelligence and good sense than most members of Congress, the army would be in a very bad condition, or rather, much worse than it is now. . . .

If we were sure of having a perfectly disinterested and patriotic man, what a good thing it would be to appoint a dictator in time of war. I begin to think I had rather have one at any rate, than see things go on as they do now.

Robert Gould Shaw's letter to his mother dated July 23, 1862.

"One of the Supreme Moments of My Existence"

Frank Holsinger was a captain in the Nineteenth Colored Infantry during the Civil War. Like many soldiers both North and South, Holsinger kept a diary of his wartime life. In it, he wrote about the blandness of daily routine as well as the excitement of battle. The following selection records his experience of being fired upon during the bloody battle of Antietam. Holsinger contemplates what gives soldiers the courage to stand firm in the face of enemy fire. Although he admits that part of him wanted to run when the bullets started flying, he attests that several factors affected his morale and influenced him to brave the danger. The combination of fear and excitement made a small fragment of time seem to Holsinger "one of the supreme moments of my existence."

The influence of a courageous man is most helpful in battle. Thus at Antietam, when surprised by the Sixth Georgia Regiment, lying immediately behind the fence at the celebrated cornfield, allowing our regiment to approach within thirty feet, and then pouring in a volley that decimated our ranks fully one-half; the regiment was demoralized. I was worse—I was stampeded. I did not expect to stop this side of the Pennsylvania line. I met a tall, thin young soldier, very boyish in manner, but cool as a cucumber . . . who yelled: "Rally, boys, rally! Die like men; don't run like dogs!" Instantly all fear vanished "Why can I not stand and take what this boy can?" I commenced loading and firing, and from this on I was as comfortable as I had been in more pleasant places.

How natural it is for a man to suppose that if a gun is discharged, he or some one is sure to be hit. He soon finds, however, that the only damage done, in ninety-nine cases out of a hundred, the only thing killed is the powder! It is not infrequently that a whole line of battle (this among raw troops) will fire upon an advancing line, and no perceptible damage ensue. They wonder how men can stand such treatment, when really they have done no damage save the terrific noise incident to the discharge. To undertake to say how many discharges are necessary to the death of a soldier in battle would be presumptuous, but I have frequently heard the remark that it took a man's weight in lead to kill him.

In presentiments of death I have no confidence. While I have seen men go into battle predicting truthfully their own death, yet I believe it is the belief of nine out of ten who go into battle that that is their last. I have never gone into battle that I did not expect to be killed. I have seen those who had no thought of death coming to them killed outright. Thus Corporal George Horton, wounded at South Mountain, wrapped his handkerchief around his wounded arm and carried the colors of our regiment to Antietam. Being asked why he did not make the best of it and go to the hospital, that he was liable to be killed, he answered, "The bullet has not [yet] been moulded to kill me." Alas! He was killed the next day.

My sensations at Antietam were a contradiction. When we were in line [passing through the woods], the boom of cannon and the hurtling shell as it crashed through the trees or exploding found its lodgment in human flesh the minies [bullets] sizzing and savagely spotting the trees; the death-like silence save the "steady men'" of our officers. The shock to the nerves were indefinable—one stands, as it were, on the brink of eternity as he goes into action. One man alone steps from the ranks and cowers behind a large tree, his nerves gone; he could go no farther. General [George] Meade sees him, and, calling a sergeant, says, "Get that man in ranks." The sergeant responds, the man refuses; General Meade rushes up with, "I'll move him!" Whipping out his saber, he deals the man a blow, he falls—who he was, I do not know. The general has no time to tarry or make inquiries. A lesson to those witnessing the scene. The whole transaction was like that of a panorama. I felt at the time the action was cruel and needless on the part of the general. I changed my mind when I became an officer, when with sword and pistol drawn to enforce discipline by keeping my men in place when going into the conflict.

When the nerves are thus unstrung, I have known relief by a silly remark. Thus at

Antietam, when in line of battle in front of the wood and exposed to a galling fire from the cornfield, standing waiting expectant with "What next?" the minies zipping by occasionally, one making the awful thud as it struck some unfortunate. As we thus stood listlessly, breathing a silent prayer, our hearts having ceased to pulsate or our minds on home and loved ones, expecting soon to be mangled or perhaps killed, some one makes an idiotic remark; thus at this time it is Mangle [one of the soldiers], in a high nasal twang, with "D——d sharp skirmishing in front." There is a laugh, it is infectious, and we are once more called back to life.

The battle when it goes your way is a different proposition. Thus having reached the east wood, each man sought a tree from behind which he not only sought protection, but dealt death to our antagonists. They halt, also seeking protection behind trees. They soon begin to retire, falling back into the cornfield. We now rush forward. We cheer; we are in ecstasies.

While shells and canister are still resonant and minies sizzing spitefully, yet I think this one of the supreme moments of my existence.

Frank Holsinger, *How Does One Feel Under Fire?* Leavenworth, KS, 1898.

The Emancipation Proclamation

Abraham Lincoln issued the Emancipation Proclamation on September 22, 1862. Federal troops had just won a victory in Maryland at the Battle of Antietam, and Lincoln saw this as an opportunity to pressure the South into rejoining the Union. The proclamation was a warning to rebellious states that if they refused to adhere to federal authority, the slaves within their dominion would be freed as of January 1, 1863. This emancipation, however, did not apply to areas of the South already under federal control or to the slaves within the border states which had not formally withdrawn from the Union. Thus, approximately 830,000 black men, women, and children remained slaves even as their brethren in the other regions of the South were legally freed.

I, Abraham Lincoln, President of the United States, by virtue of the power in me vested as Commander-in-Chief of the Army and Navy of the United States in time of actual armed rebellion against the authority and government of the United States, and as a fit and necessary war measure for suppressing said rebellion, do, on this 1st day of January, A.D. 1863, and in accordance with my purpose so to do, publicly proclaimed for the full period of one hundred days from the first day above mentioned, order and designate as the States and parts of States wherein the people thereof, respectively, are this day in rebellion against the United States the following, to wit:

Arkansas, Texas, Louisiana (except the parishes of St. Bernard, Plaquemines, Jefferson, St. John, St. Charles, St. James, Ascension, Assumption, Terrebonne, Lafourche, St. Mary, St. Martin, and Orleans, including

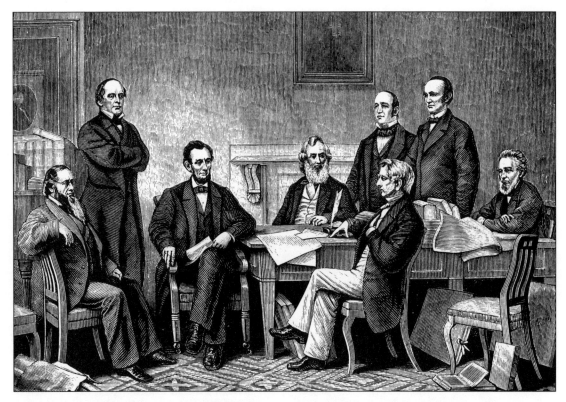

To pressure the South into rejoining the Union, President Lincoln signs the Emancipation Proclamation, granting freedom to Confederate slaves.

the city of New Orleans), Mississippi, Alabama, Florida, Georgia, South Carolina, North Carolina, and Virginia (except for the forty-eight counties designated as West Virginia, and also the counties of Berkeley, Accomac, Northhampton, Elizabeth City, York, Princess Anne, and Norfolk, including the cities of Norfolk and Portsmouth), and which excepted parts are for the present left precisely as if this proclamation were not issued.

And by virtue of the power and for the purpose aforesaid, I do order and declare that all persons held as slaves within said designated States and parts of States are, and henceforward shall be, free; and that the Executive Government of the United States, including the military and naval authorities thereof, will recognize and maintain the freedom of said persons.

And I hereby enjoin upon the people so declared to be free to abstain from all violence, unless in necessary self-defense; and I recommend to them that, in all cases when allowed, they labor faithfully for reasonable wages.

And I further declare and make known that such persons of suitable condition will be received into the armed service of the United States to garrison forts, positions, stations, and other places, and to man vessels of all sorts in said service.

And upon this act, sincerely believed to be an act of justice, warranted by the Constitution upon military necessity, I invoke the considerate judgment of mankind and the gracious favor of Almighty God.

Abraham Lincoln, Emancipation Proclamation, September 22, 1862.

"Are We Soldiers, or Are We Labourers?"

Although two congressional acts and the Emancipation Proclamation declared that black soldiers could serve in the Union army, none of these measures guaranteed the eager recruits would be treated equally. Black soldiers had to serve in all-black combat regiments, they received lower pay ($10 minus $3 for clothing expenses, while white soldiers earned $13 plus $3.50 for clothing), and they could not earn an officer's rank. As these black regiments proved themselves in battle, however, many individual soldiers began asking why they were discriminated against when they were risking their lives in the defense of their country. Some, like James Henry Gooding of the all-black 54th Massachusetts Regiment, took their complaints to the highest office, petitioning Abraham Lincoln to explain the discrepancy.

Your Excellency, Abraham Lincoln:

Your Excellency will pardon the presumption of an humble individual like myself, in addressing you, but the earnest Solicitation of my Comrades in Arms beside the genuine interest felt by myself in the matter is my excuse, for placing before the Executive head of the Nation our Common Grievance. On the 6th of the last Month, the Paymaster of the department informed us, that if we would decide to receive the sum of $10 (ten dollars) per month, he would come and pay us that sum, but that, on the sitting of Congress, the Reg. would, in his opinion, be allowed the other 3 (three). He did not give us any guarantee that this would be, as he hoped; certainly he had no authority for making any such guarantee, and we cannot suppose him acting in any way interested.

Now the main question is, Are we *Soldiers*, or are we *Labourers?* We are fully armed, and equipped, have done all the various Duties pertaining to a Soldier's life, have conducted ourselves to the complete satisfaction of General Officers, who were, if any[thing], prejudiced *against* us, but who now accord us all the encouragement and honour due us; have shared the perils and Labour of Reducing the first stronghold that flaunted a Traitor Flag; and more, Mr. President. Today the Anglo-Saxon Mother, Wife, or Sister are not alone in tears for departed Sons, Husbands and Brothers. The patient, trusting Descendants of Afric's Clime have dyed the ground with blood, in defense of the Union, and Democracy. Men, too, your Excellency, who know in a measure the cruelties of the Iron heel of oppression, which in years gone by, the very Power their blood is now being spilled to maintain, ever ground them to the dust.

But when the war trumpet sounded o'er the land, when men knew not the Friend from the Traitor, the Black man laid his life at the Altar of the Nation,—and he was refused. When the arms of the Union were beaten, in the first year of the War, and the Executive called more food for its ravaging maw, again the black man begged the privilege of aiding his Country in her need, to be again refused.

And now he is in the War, and how has he conducted himself? Let their dusky forms rise up, out [of] the mires of James Island, and give the answer. Let the rich mould around [Fort] Wagner's parapets be upturned, and there will be found an Eloquent answer. Obedient and patient and Solid as a wall are they. All we lack is a paler hue and a better acquaintance with the Alphabet. Now your Excellency, we have done a Soldier's Duty. Why Can't we have a Soldier's pay?

We appeal to you, Sir, as the Executive of the Nation, to have us justly Dealt with. The Regt. do pray that they be assured their ser-

Freed slaves proudly pose for a photo as newly appointed Union soldiers in the 107th Colored Infantry.

vice will be fairly appreciated by paying them as American *Soldiers*, not as menial hirelings.

Black men, you may well know, are poor; three dollars per month for a year will supply their needy Wives and little ones with fuel. If you, as Chief Magistrate of the Nation, will assure us of our whole pay, we are content. Our Patriotism, our enthusiasm will have a new impetus, to exert our energy more and more to aid our Country. Not that our hearts have ever flagged in Devotion, spite the evident apathy displayed in our behalf, but We feel as though our Country spurned us, now that we are sworn to serve her. Please give this a moment's attention.

James Henry Gooding

Letter of James Henry Gooding to Abraham Lincoln, 1863.

Susan B. Anthony (left) and Elizabeth Cady Stanton crusaded for the abolition of slavery and later for women's rights.

A Call for Loyal Women

Elizabeth Cady Stanton and Susan B. Anthony were pioneers in the early women's rights movement and the abolitionist crusade. At the outbreak of war, they agreed to curtail their feminist activism and support the Union war effort. By 1863, however, both Stanton and Anthony had grown dissatisfied by the limited role Northern women could play in the Union cause. They were also displeased with President Lincoln's Emancipation Proclamation. Like many antislavery advocates, they believed the decree did not go far enough in destroying the evil institution of slavery. In May of that year, Stanton and Anthony helped form the Women's National Loyal League which petitioned Congress to enact laws to abolish slavery. The following call for this meeting of loyal women reveals that Stanton and Anthony had not only the end of slavery in mind but the furthering of women's political power in the new, free nation.

In this crisis of our country's destiny, it is the duty of every citizen to consider the peculiar blessings of a republican form of government, and decide what sacrifices of wealth and life are demanded for its defence and preservation. The policy of the war, our whole future life, depends on a clearly-defined idea of the end proposed, and the immense advantages to be secured to ourselves and all mankind, by its accomplishment. No mere party or sectional cry, no technicalities of Constitution or military law, no mottoes of craft or policy are big enough to touch the great heart of a nation in the midst of revolution. A grand idea, such as freedom or justice, is needful to kindle and sustain the fires of a high enthusiasm.

At this hour, the best word and work of every man and woman are imperatively demanded. To man, by common consent, is assigned the forum, camp, and field. What is woman's legitimate work, and how she may best accomplish it, is worthy our earnest counsel one with another. We have heard many complaints of the lack of enthusiasm among Northern women; but, when a mother lays her son on the altar of her country, she asks an object equal to the sacrifice. In nursing the sick and wounded, knitting socks, scraping lint, and making jellies, the bravest and best may weary if the thoughts mount not in faith to something beyond and above it all. Work is worship only when a noble purpose fills the soul. Woman is equally interested and responsible with man in the final settlement of this problem of self-government; therefore let none stand idle spectators now. When every hour is big with destiny, and each delay but complicates our difficulties, it is high time for the daughters of the revolution, in solemn council, to unseal the last will and testament of the Fathers—lay hold of their birthright of freedom, and keep it a sacred trust for all coming generations.

Elizabeth Cady Stanton and Susan B. Anthony, "Call for a Meeting of the Loyal Women of the Nation," 1863.

Smite the Copperheads

Proslavery sentiment remained strong in parts of the North during the war years. People who held these views were known as Copperheads, after the deadly snake of that name. The Copperheads were a force to be reckoned with, especially in Pennsylvania, where they clashed in bloody feuds with abolitionists. When the issue of allowing blacks into the Union army arose in 1863, the Copperheads came out to discourage blacks from enlisting and generally discredit their fighting abilities in the minds of the white public. Antislavery advocates, however, were just as determined to aid black recruitment. In this April 1863 letter to the Weekly Anglo-African, *a leading journal of black affairs, George E. Stephens, a future enlistee with the all-black 54th Massachusetts Regiment, describes the base tactics of the Copperheads. He further argues that it is important to black pride for able men to enlist, fight for freedom and honor, and ultimately smite the Copperheads and their false claims.*

I am right glad that the black brigade is rolling up so bright a record. May they continue to drive before them the buzzard foe!

You meet these copperheads at every step, and when violence is not resorted to, they come [with] the friendship and counsellor dodge. They ask, "Are you going to enlist in the army?" Of course, you answer "Yes!" They continue, "Any colored gentleman who will go down South to fight is a fool. Every one of them that the rebels catch will be hanged, or sent into the Indigo mines, or cut up into mincemeat, or quartered and pickled, or spitted, or—or—What good is it going to do the colored people to go fight and lose their lives? Better stay home and keep out of harm's way."

These are the arguments that the copperheads insinuate into the ears of the credulous, the ignorant, and the timid. They do not tell you that the measure of the slaveholder's iniquity is completed; that the accumulated wrongs of two centuries are a thousand-fold more horrible than two centuries of war and massacre. They do not tell you that it were "better to die free, than live slaves"—that your wronged and outraged sisters and brethren are calling on you to take up arms and place your interests and your lives in the balance against their oppressors—that "your dead fathers speak to you from their graves," or "Heaven, as with a voice of thunder, calls on you to arise from the dust," and smite with an avenging hand the obdurate, cruel, and relentless enemy and traitor, who has trampled in the dust the flag of his country and whose life and sacred honor are pledged to wage an interminable war against your race.

Oh no, to tell us these truths would be to nerve our arms and fire our hearts for the noble struggle for country and liberty. Men and brethren! for the sake of honor, manhood and courage—in the name of God, of country, and of race, spit upon the base sycophants who thus dare to insult you.

George E. Stephens, letter to editor, *Weekly Anglo-African*, April 11, 1863.

Northern Draft Riots

When Congress passed the Enrollment Act of 1863, the federal government effectively took the job of recruiting soldiers away from the states. The institution of a national draft was not met with sympathy by a Northern populace that believed its civil liberties were at stake. In New York, the reception was especially bitter. Having just swallowed the controversial Emancipation Proclamation that allowed the enlistment of black troops, New Yorkers faced with conscription attacked draft offices and rioted through the city's streets in July 1863. Other Northerners understood the outrage but deplored the rioting. In this pamphlet from Rhode Island, an anonymous author argues that although the draft is illegal and unconstitutional, he is shocked at the violent response in some Northern cities.

The riotous demonstrations recently witnessed in New York and some other places, which have been occasioned by the Draft, are much to be deplored by all classes of citizens. No circumstances can justify such terrible proceedings, and their authors can offer no sufficient excuse for their conduct. But now, when the madness of the

Outraged citizens riot in the streets of New York as a result of the Civil War draft.

hour seems to have subsided, at least for the present, it may be wise for both people and rulers, to view the subject candidly and carefully. The public felt aggrieved by the proceedings under the conscription act; they felt that a great wrong had been done them; they murmured in secret and in public, and the disturbances which we have witnessed were only the outcroppings of one universal indignation. That the people were not right in resorting to violent means to redress a wrong, is everywhere acknowledged; but whether they or the government most deserve censure is a question. It seems to us that well informed, far seeing men might have anticipated such results from such legislation. If men are wanted for the army, the government should endeavor to raise them by constitutional and legitimate means. A very brief examination of the question should be sufficient to convince any unbiassed enquirer that Congress had no constitutional right to pass the obnoxious conscription act. The constitution of the United States confers no such authority upon Congress. And the uniform conduct of the government, both in war and peace, before the passing of this conscription act, clearly shows that no such power was delegated or intended to be delegated to Congress. . . .

But an attempt is made to justify the existing conscription act, on the ground that the war in which we are engaged at the present time, is not a foreign war, but only an insurrection, and therefore Congress has a right to use the militia to suppress it. In answer to this it may be said that this is no such insurrection or invasion as the constitution contemplates; 'tis no mob, nor riot, nor temporary insurrection to be suppressed by a hasty appeal to the militia. But it is open war of mammoth proportions, against an organized government, recognized by all Europe, and by our intercourse with its authorities, as a belligerent power, having in all respects the character of a foreign enemy, and however unwilling we may be to acknowledge the fact, we are compelled to treat this enemy, not as a band of insurgents, but precisely as we should an English or French army. The present conflict is either a war in the fullest sense of the term, or no war at all, but simply an insurrection. The president claims that it is a war, and therefore he is authorized to suspend the writ of habeas corpus and do many other things which he would not be authorized to do in case of an insurrection only. Now if he is right in this, the conscription act is unconstitutional, and the president has no authority to enforce it. Much more might be said to show that this act and all proceedings under it are unauthorized by the Constitution of the United States, and in a legal sense absolutely void, but we have no time to pursue the investigation further. Whenever an appeal is made to the proper tribunal, it will undoubtedly be declared unconstitutional.

The Draft, or, Conscription Reviewed by the People, anonymous pamphlet from Providence, Rhode Island in 1863.

The Choctaw Support the Confederacy

Native American tribes living on lands within the Confederacy and the border states were often caught up in the conflict that surrounded them. Many of these tribes had suffered relocation and broken promises from the federal government and were therefore inclined to help the South. Some sent warriors to fight in the Confederate armies with the hope that the Confederate government would redress some of the wrongs of the past. Jefferson Davis's government, however, was just as lax in fulfilling promises as the treaty makers in Washington. In this letter dated October 21, 1863, P.P. Pitchlynn, the head of the Choctaw Nation, reaffirms his tribe's commitment to the Southern cause. Yet couched within his reassurances are hints that if his tribe is continually treated with "indifference and neglect," the Choctaw may be forced to negotiate with the Lincoln government.

Col. Eakin—Editor Telegraph—Dear sir: Inasmuch as reports are in circulation prejudicial to me as a Southern man and Choctaw, I solicit a place in your columns that I may place myself right before your public. I am represented by some as a Union man, by others as favoring a treaty of union with the Lincoln Government, and by others as being, at best, lukewarm in the Southern cause. To these several reports I can truthfully affirm that there is no truth in them whatever. As regards the first point in the charge, I reply that I am a Southern man by birth, education, association and interest. As to favoring or suggesting a treaty with the Lincoln Government, the charge is as untrue as it is unjust or impracticable. We have consulted with each other in regard to our situation. The Federal forces were advancing without opposition—destruction and desolation following in their wake. What is to be the fate of the Choctaw people if their neighbors and friends from Arkansas and Texas forsake them in this their day of trial and gloom? Reports were current that the white forces would be withdrawn from this department. Will the Confederates leave them to the Federal mercy and merciless jayhawkers? This Nation is the only abiding place for the poor Choctaws. For unlike the white man, there are no sister States to which he can emigrate. In view of such state of affairs, it was suggested, as the last resort, that permission be solicited of the Confederate States for the Choctaws to make an armistice. But in no instance, and under no conditions whatever, did the Choctaws intend to switch without the consent of the Confederate States; nor did they intend to act on that suggestion only as a means of preserving a home for the poor Choctaws, and, also, as securing a temporary abiding place to those unfortunates of other tribes amongst us. But so long as our neighbors and allies stood by us in defense of our common cause, I have urged, in speeches to the Choctaws, that they should unitedly peril their lives and their all in defence of the South. If I have appeared lukewarm, it has grown out of denunciations which the interference in the affairs of this department by Confederate commanders, unconnected with it, have provoked. It is well known that arms, clothing and money intended for the Indian allies were used elsewhere. Such interference has caused the Indian allies to think that they were treated with indifference and neglect. And it also greatly embarrassed the commanders in this department in their operations against the enemy. Had I been a Union man, these things would have passed with indifference; but a desire to see justice done the Choctaw people cause me to "cry aloud and spare not." Furthermore, the constitution of my mind and not its convictions may have caused me to appear lukewarm to the casual observer; yet while others have been hot I have been warm; while some have been blatant for Southern rights I have been consistent and hopeful; while some have professed zeal for the cause and love for its defenders I have furnished sons for the battle, kept an open door and free table for the Southern soldiers. My desire to sustain my consistency before the better class of Southern people induces me to thus publicly notice and give character to irresponsible reports.

Very respectfully,
P.P. Pitchlynn

Head of Choctaw Nation Reaffirms His Tribe's Position, October 21, 1863.

The Burning of Chambersburg

When Confederate armies marched into Pennsylvania in 1864, it was the first and only large scale invasion of the North during the Civil War. While many Southern cities and towns had witnessed destruction or Union occupation from the outset of the war, their Northern counterparts had, for the most part, not suffered such hardships. Yet when General Robert E. Lee moved his forces toward Gettysburg, towns along the invasion route understood what it was like to have a enemy army in their midst.

In Chambersburg, Pennsylvania, Rachel Cormany recorded what it was like when Confederate troops marched on the town and demanded a ransom. Since the town could not pay, the Southerners set fire to many of the buildings before angrily moving on.

August 6, 1864. Just a week this morning the rebels turned up in our devoted town again. Before they entered they roused us out of our slumbers by throwing two shells in. This was between 3 and 4 A.M. by 5—the gray back hordes came pouring in. They demanded 500,000 dollars in default of which the town would be burned—They were told that it was impossible to raise that amount—The reb's then came down to 100,000 in gold which was just as impossible. When they were informed of the impossibility they deliberately went from house to house & fired it. The whole heart of the town is burned. They gave no time for people to get any thing out. Each had to escape for life & took only what they could first grab. Some saved considerable. Others only the clothes on their backs—& even some of those were taken off as they escaped from their burning dwellings. O! the 30th July 1864 was a sad day to the people of Chambersburg. In most of cases where the buildings were left money was paid. They were here too but we talked them out of it. We told them we were widows & that saved us here. About 3000 were made homeless in less than three hours. This whole week has been one of great excitement. We live in constant dread. I never spent such days as these few last I never spent—I feel as if I could not stay in this country longer. I feel quite sick of the dread & excitement.

James C. Mohr, ed., *The Cormany Diaries: A Northern Family in the Civil War.* Pittsburgh: University of Pittsburgh Press, 1982.

The Gettysburg Address

With Union armies rampaging through Virginia, Confederate general Robert E. Lee decided to invade the North in hopes of drawing the Union soldiers out of the South and relieving the suffering visited upon his home state. In early July Lee met newly appointed General George Meade at Gettysburg, Pennsylvania. There, from July 1 through July 3, raged one of the most spectacular battles in American history. Ultimately Lee's army did not prevail and the Confederates were forced to return to the South, never again to invade Northern soil. Gettysburg was the high water mark for the Confederacy. Although the South would struggle on for two more years, they would fight a losing war.

On November 19, Abraham Lincoln helped dedicate the cemetery at Gettysburg for the soldiers of both armies who died there. While his was not the only speech given that day, it was the shortest. Lincoln was careful not to exploit the Union victory and alienate the South from potential reconciliation. Instead his eloquent words spoke of the sacrifices made at Gettysburg in the service of keeping American democracy intact.

Four score and seven years ago our fathers brought forth upon this continent a new nation, conceived in Liberty, and dedicated to the proposition that all men are created equal.

Now we are engaged in a great civil war, testing whether that nation or any nation so conceived and so dedicated can long endure. We are met on a great battlefield of

President Lincoln delivers the Gettysburg Address, commemorating the soldiers killed at Gettysburg and calling on the living to preserve a democratic Union.

that war. We have come to dedicate a portion of that field as a final resting place for those who here gave their lives that that nation might live. It is altogether fitting and proper that we should do this.

But in a larger sense we cannot dedicate—we cannot consecrate—we cannot hallow—this ground. The brave men, living and dead, who struggled here, have consecrated it, far above our poor power to add or detract. The world will little note nor long remember what we say here, but it can never forget what they did here. It is for us the living, rather, to be dedicated here to the unfinished work which they who fought here have thus far so nobly advanced. It is rather for us to be here dedicated to the great task remaining before us—that from these honored dead we take increased devotion to that cause for which they gave the last full measure of devotion—that we here highly resolve that these dead shall not have died in vain—that this nation, under God, shall have a new birth of freedom—and that government of the people, by the people, for the people, shall not perish from the earth.

Abraham Lincoln, "Gettysburg Address," November 19, 1863.

A Confederate Soldier's Conviction

Although in 1863 the South had suffered a defeat at Gettysburg in the east and the Union's new fighting general, Ulysses S. Grant, was garnering victories in the west, Confederate soldiers were not ready to give up the fight. To many Southerners, Lincoln's freeing of the slaves only made public what they had always known: The aim of Northern aggression was the destruction of slavery and Southern culture. This steeled Southern convictions. As this December 31, 1863, letter from Edmund DeWitt Patterson, a Confederate prisoner of war, attests, the South would continue to fight against the "abolition government" to the bitter end.

Now, I am a prisoner of war on the little island of Lake Erie [Johnson's Island, near Sandusky, Ohio], and with a prospect before me anything but cheering; entirely separated and cut off from the outside world, unable to take any active part in the struggle which is still going on between justice and injustice, right and wrong, freedom and oppression, unable to strike a blow in the glorious cause of Southern independence.

Now, the end of the war seems more distant than ever. Time only shows on the part of the abolition government a firmer determination than ever to subjugate; while on the other hand time only shows on the part of the South a stronger determination to fight to the bitter end, trusting alone to the god of battles for success at last. And we *will* succeed. Who will say that a country such as ours, rich in everything that makes a nation great and prosperous, a country with broad valleys unequalled in fertility by any others upon which the sun shines, a country abounding in natural fortresses and inhabited by eight millions of brave people determined to be free and willing to sacrifice everything even life itself upon the altar of their country, united as no people ever were before, I ask, who will say, in view of all this, that the South will not be free. I engaged in this war firmly believing that the South would be successful and now after nearly three years of war, I find that time has only served to strengthen that opinion. I believe that winter will pass and spring come again with its verdure and flowers—I believe it as I believe anything that I see around me, the fair fields of the South may be transformed into deserts, and the places where now may be seen stately edifices, tokens of wealth and refinement, may be made as howling wildernesses, Yankee hirelings may occupy every state, every County in the South, they may occupy our state capitols and our seaport towns,—but our hill tops and hollows,—never. We will carry on the war even there.

Edmund DeWitt Patterson, *Yankee Rebel: The Civil War Journal of Edmund DeWitt Patterson.* Chapel Hill: University of North Carolina Press, 1966.

A Confederate Act to Employ Free Blacks and Slaves

As the South was resolved to resist the "abolition government" of the North, it faced a severe crisis in manpower in 1863 that forced it to enact extraordinary measures. Needing all able-bodied white men to fight against the encroaching Union armies, Jefferson Davis and the Confederate congress put forth a bill on January 5, 1864, to conscript free blacks in the South to work for the war effort. The bill also provided for the impressment of slaves for these duties if the owners were compensated in lost wages. The resulting act, passed on March 14, provoked much controversy among Southerners who saw no need for using blacks in any capacity to fight a white man's war.

Whereas, the efficiency of the army is greatly diminished by the withdrawal from the ranks of able-bodied soldiers to set as teamsters, and in various other capacities in which free negroes and slaves might be advantageously employed; therefore,

SEC 1. The Congress of the Confederate States of America do enact, That all male free negroes resident in the Confederate States, between the ages of eighteen and fifty years, shall be held liable to perform such duties with the army, or in connection with the military defenses of the country, in the way of work upon fortification, or in Government work, for the production or preparation of material of war, or in military hospitals, as the Secretary of War may from time to time prescribe; and while engaged in the performance of such duties shall receive rations and clothing, and compensation at the rate of eleven dollars a month, under such rules and regulations as the said Secretary may establish: Provided, That the Secretary of War, with the approval of the President, may exempt from the operations of this act such free Negroes as the interests of the country may require should be exempted, or such as he may think proper to exempt on grounds of justice, equity, or necessity.

SEC 2. Be it further enacted, That the Secretary of War is hereby authorized to employ for duties similar to those indicated in the preceding section of this act, as many male negro slaves, not to exceed [gap in the text] in his judgement, the wants of the service may require, furnishing them while so employed with proper rations and clothing, under rules and regulations to be established by him, and paying to the owners of said slaves wages at the rate of eleven dollars per month for their use and service, and in the event of the loss of any slaves, while so employed, by the act of the enemy, or by disease incurred, in consequence of the discharge of any service required of said slaves, then by the owners of the same shall be entitled to receive the full value of such slaves, to be paid under such rules and regulations as the Secretary of War may establish.

SEC 3. Be it further enacted, That when the Secretary of War shall be unable to procure the services of slaves in any military department in sufficient numbers for the necessities of the department upon the terms and conditions set forth in the preceding section, then he is hereby authorized to impress the services of as many slaves as may be required from time to time to discharge the duties indicated in the first section of this act, under such rules and regulations as the said Secretary may establish: Provided, That slaves so impressed shall, while employed, receive the same rations and clothing in kind and quantity as slaves regularly hired from their owners, and in the event of their loss, shall be paid for in the same manner, and under the same rules and regulations as those who may have been hired.

"An Act to Increase the Efficiency of the Army by the Employment of Free Negroes and Slaves in Certain Capacities," House Bill read in the Confederate House of Representatives on January 5, 1864.

★ Chapter 4 ★

The End of the Confederacy

In February 1862 Forts Donelson and Henry in Tennessee fell to Union troops. The commander of the federal assault was Ulysses S. Grant, a promising leader who had recently been promoted to general. Grant's fame as a general began at Fort Donelson when he refused to discuss lenient surrender terms with the Confederate defenders. He was a soldier who believed his duty was to carry out his president's orders to suppress the rebellion by any means necessary.

In his next major battle at Shiloh, Tennessee, Grant eked out a marginal victory. His army was taken by surprise, and Confederates pushed the Union lines back with heavy casualties before Union reserves arrived and held the Confederates from further advances. Grant's setback provoked censure from many of his military colleagues who hinted to President Abraham Lincoln that perhaps Grant should be relieved of command. Lincoln reportedly countered this unwelcome counsel by saying, "I can't spare this man—he fights." Indeed, Grant seemed to be the kind of fighting general Lincoln had been searching for since the war's beginning. He was a tenacious leader who was willing to engage the enemy and continue to fight him even through reversals of fortune.

Grant's reputation grew as time wore on. He achieved several important victories in the Trans-Mississippi West that significantly quieted that theater of war. In March 1864, Lincoln gave Grant command over all Union armies in hopes he had found a match for the Confederate's brilliant tactician, Robert E. Lee, who had been so successful in defeating federal troops in the east. Throughout 1864 and 1865 Grant and Lee faced off, with Lee taking much of the losses but still keeping Grant from achieving his objectives. The stalemate and resulting casualty rates worried Washington, but Lincoln stood behind his new general.

Both Lincoln and Grant knew the Union had the advantages. Grant and Lee were talented strategists with strong wills, but by 1865 Lee was suffering severe handicaps in the contest. Southern ports had been completely cut off by a federal blockade and supplies were hard to come by. Furthermore, Lee's army was dwindling and could not acquire the numbers of reinforcements that seemingly streamed into the Northern forces. Since Grant was willing to exploit Northern industrial and manpower advantages, he could fight a war of attrition that would wear down the South. Finally, because of the North's superiority in numbers, Grant had several armies that he could use to run rampant through the South. One such command, under the leadership of another hard-bitten general, William T. Sherman, marched nearly unopposed through Georgia, wreaking destruction in a key Confederate state that had long been spared the ravages of war.

On April 9, 1865, General Lee's army was pushed into a corner and its commander recognized the futility of continuing the war of attrition. He had barely fifty thousand men left under his command while Grant had more than twice that number. At Appomattox Court House in Virginia, Lee surrendered the proud but beaten Army of Northern Virginia. Within two months, the remaining Confederate forces that were scattered from Texas to North Carolina followed suit. The great American Civil War was over, and the South awaited the bitter period of Reconstruction that did little to heal old wounds in the nation.

"Unconditional Surrender" Grant

In 1862, Ulysses S. Grant was a brigadier general in the Trans-Mississippi theater. In that year, he was given the task of seizing Forts Henry and Donelson in Tennessee. Within two weeks time, Grant's force captured both forts, a remarkable feat. At the capitulation of Fort Donelson, the Confederate defenders asked for lenient terms, but Grant would not negotiate and called for unconditional surrender. His hard bargaining earned him the nickname of "Unconditional Surrender" Grant among his men. More importantly, word of this tough, fighting general reached Abraham Lincoln who—desperate for aggressive leaders—promoted him first to the commander of the Department of Tennessee in 1863, and then to commander of the entire Northern army in 1864.

In this excerpt from an 1862 Chicago Tribune *article, Grant's legend is born in the official exchanges between Grant and General S.B. Buckner, the commander of the Confederate troops defending Fort Donelson.*

Headquarters Fort Donelson, February 16, 1862.

To Brig. Gen. U.S. Grant, Con'g U.S. forces near Fort Donelson. . . .

Sir: In consideration of all the circumstances governing the present situation of affairs at this station, I propose to the commanding officer of the Federal forces, the appointment of Commissioners to agree upon terms of capitulation of the forces and post under my command, and in that view suggest an armistice until 2 o'clock to-day.

At the Battle of Fort Donelson, Ulysses S. Grant's soldiers overwhelmed the Confederate troops, demanding and winning an unconditional surrender.

Headquarters Army in the Field, near Donelson, Feb. 16, 1862.

To Gen. S.B. Buckner, Confederate Army—

No terms except unconditional and immediate surrender can be accepted. I propose to move immediately upon your words.

I am, sir, very respectfully,

Your obd't serv't,

U.S. Grant, Brig. Gen. Commanding.

Headquarters, Dover, Tenn., Feb. 16, 1862.

To Brig. Gen. U.S. Grant, U.S.A.:

Sir: The distribution of the forces under my command, incident to an unexpected change of commanders and the overwhelming force under your command, compel me, notwithstanding the brilliant success of the Confederate arms yesterday, to accept the ungenerous and unchivalrous terms which you propose. I am, dear sir,

Your very obedient servant,

S.B. Buckner, Brig. Con. C.S.A.

"The Capture of Fort Donelson," *Chicago Tribune*, 1862.

I am, sir, very respectfully,

Your obedient servant,

S.B. Buckner, Brig. Gen. C.S.A.

"The Eve of Stirring Events"

Northern newspapers in 1861 were pleased to extol the strength of the Union and the inevitably quick defeat of secessionists. However, as Southern resolve proved itself and casualties mounted, the editorials became less optimistic and more realistic about the slow progress of the war. In 1864, the Chicago Tribune *published the following article that spoke of a coming battle of great significance. However, instead of forecasting a decisive victory, the paper cautioned its readers to be prepared for inconclusive engagements that would be part of a larger campaign of attrition. Ulysses S. Grant, believing he was no longer saddled with the unrealistic expectations to win the war quickly, decided the mood was right to launch a campaign in Virginia that was designed to wear away at Confederate resolve and manpower, bringing a distant but ultimate victory to the North.*

That we are now upon the eve of stirring events is apparent enough. The state of the season, the condition of the opposing armies, and the demands and expectations of the country, all look to active hostilities without much more of delay. The enemy are hurrying up all their spare men to the front—especially into Virginia; having settled it in their minds that the contest is to be there. In the meantime several things seems to be generally assumed by us as sure to happen—all of which may or may not occur. One thing, upon which there seems to be no reason of doubt is, that some one great battle, in which all the Virginia army is to take part, is to come off; and then, in the second place, that this battle will decide the contest. It is true enough that such a thing is possible, and it cannot be said improbable, yet it is well not to be too positive in our expectations. . . . Suppose us to have a battle, or two of them, of considerable magnitude, they may not be at once decisive. It has been an expectation held out from the very beginning of the war, that it was to come to an end at once. It was to be ended at first in a month, then in a campaign; and thus from period to period expectation has been led forward; of course to be disappointed. One hope now is to grind the enemy's army to powder. But in that grinding, it is to be expected that we ourselves will suffer some grinding also. They that wield the sword are liable, of necessity, to perish with it. We may have to do a good deal of fighting before the relative strength of the opposing armies, at present existing, is destroyed; and this may wear away the season till the heats of midsummer forbid active field operations; and thus the spring campaign may verge over into one which shall consume the autumn months. . . .

Be not too positive as to this or that; but in the determination to fight out this rebellion, let there be no relaxing; be it a month or a week or years that shall be necessary to end it.

"What Is to Happen?" *Chicago Tribune* editorial, 1864.

Grant at Spotsylvania

Once Ulysses S. Grant was given command of all Union armies, he planned to work around the Confederate armies in the east and destroy their supply bases, reducing their ability to continue the war. Unfortunately, General Robert E. Lee was a resourceful and capable strategist himself, and Grant's campaign quickly bogged down into a series of inconclusive yet costly fights. In Northern newspapers, the man who was once lauded as "Unconditional Surrender" Grant was now lambasted as "Grant the Butcher."

Still, Lee's armies, though not defeated, suffered from attrition, and dwindling numbers of troops it could not replace made the South's future prospects look grim. In May, 1864, at the Battle of Spotsylvania Court House in Virginia, Lee successfully held off Grant's army, but he lost ten thousand men in the effort. Grant lost seventeen thousand men and withdrew from the battle. In this May 13 letter to his wife, Julia, Grant had yet to give up the contest and writes with optimism that the Confederate army will soon break.

Dear Julia,

The ninth day of battle is just closing with victory so far on our side. But the enemy are fighting with great desperation entrenching themselves in every position they take up. We have lost many thousand men killed and wounded and the enemy have no doubt lost more. We have taken about eight thousand prisoners and lost likely three thousand. Among our wounded the great majority are but slightly hurt but most of them will be unfit for service in this battle. I have reinforcements now coming up which will greatly

Ulysses S. Grant reads a letter from his wife, Julia.

encourage our men and discourage the enemy correspondingly.

I am very well and full of hope. I see from the papers the country is also hopeful.

Remember me to your father and Aunt Fanny. Kisses for yourself and the children. The world has never seen so bloody or so protracted a battle as the one being fought and I hope never will again. The enemy were really whipped yesterday but their situation is desperate beyond anything heretofore known. To loose this battle they loose their cause. As bad as it is they have fought for it with a gallantry worthy of a better.

Ulys.

Ulysses S. Grant, Letter to his Wife, May 13, 1864.

Farragut's Victory at Mobile Bay

While Union armies closed in on the Confederate capital at Richmond, the U.S. Navy sealed off the remaining Southern supply ports along the Gulf of Mexico. Rear Admiral David Farragut commanded the fleet that would assault the South's last port city of Mobile, Alabama, in 1864. With his squadron deployed for battle, Farragut weighed the enemy's defenses. Mobile was protected by fortresses and gunboats along the shore, but perhaps more dangerous were the torpedoes (mines) that were floating at the entrance to the port. Full of bravado and having no options, Farragut gave the order to attack on August 5. Just as the Union fleet entered the harbor, the ironclad Tecumseh *struck a mine and exploded. Unwilling to disengage, Farragut, aboard his flagship, the* Hartford, *gave the legendary command, "Damn the torpedoes! Full speed ahead." His fleet carried the day and closed off the last of the Southern ports. This excerpt from his report to the Navy Department captures some of the action of the battle as Farragut and his ships take on the Confederate gunboat, the* Tennessee.

I steamed through between the buoys, where the torpedoes were supposed to have been sunk. These buoys had been previously examined by my flag-lieutenant, J. Crittenden Watson, in several nightly reconnaissances. Though he had not been able to discover the sunken torpedoes, yet we had been assured by refugees, deserters, and others, of their existence, but believing that, from their having been some time in the water they were probably innocuous, I determined to take the chance of their explosion. From the moment I turned to the northwestward, to clear the middle ground, we were enabled to keep such a broadside fire upon the batteries of Fort Morgan that their guns did us comparatively little injury.

"Just after we passed the fort, which was about ten minutes before eight o'clock, the ram "Tennessee" dashed out at this ship, as had been expected, and in anticipation of which I had ordered the monitors on our starboard side. I took no further notice of her than to return her fire. . . .

Having passed the fort and dispersed the enemy's gunboats, I had ordered most of the vessels to anchor, when I perceived the ram "Tennessee" standing up for this

Rear Admiral David Farragut (top right), commander of the Hartford, *leads his crew through a line of floating mines to take the Confederate gunboat,* Tennessee.

ship. This was at forty-five minutes past eight. I was not long in comprehending his intentions to be the destruction of the flagship. The monitors, and such of the wooden vessels as I thought best adapted for the purpose, were immediately ordered to attack the ram, not only with their guns, but bows on at full speed, and then began one of the fiercest naval combats on record.

The "Monongahela," Commander Strong, was the first vessel that struck her, and in doing so carried away his own prow, together with the cutwater, without apparently doing her adversary much injury. The "Lackawanna," Captain Marchand, was the next vessel to strike her, which she did at full speed; but though her stern was cut and crushed to the plank ends for the distance of three feet above the water's edge to five feet below, the only perceptible effect on the ram was to give her a heavy list.

The "Hartford" was the third vessel which struck her, but, as the "Tennessee" quickly shifted her helm, the blow was a glancing one, and as she rasped along our side, we poured our whole port broadside of nine-inch solid shot within ten feet of her casement. The monitors worked slowly, but delivered their fire as opportunity offered. The "Chickasaw" succeeded in getting under her stern, and a fifteen-inch shot from the "Manhattan" broke through her iron plating and heavy wooden backing though the missile itself did not enter the vessel.

Immediately after the collision with the flagship, I directed Captain Drayton to bear down for the ram again. He was doing so at full speed when, unfortunately, the "Lackawanna" ran into the "Hartford" just forward of the mizzen-mast, cutting her down to within two feet of the water's edge. We soon got clear again, however, and were fast approaching our adversary, when she struck her colors and ran up the white flag.

David G. Farragut, Report on the Battle of Mobile Bay, Alabama, made to the Department of the Navy in August 1864.

Atlanta Begs General Sherman for Mercy

From August through December 1864, General William T. Sherman headed his Union army into Georgia. Starting in the northwest corner and ending in Savannah on the coast, Sherman led his troops on a rampage through Georgia, a rebel state that had yet to experience warfare within its borders. Ignoring the Southern army that was trying to distract him from carrying out his plan, Sherman's men burned plantations, tore up railroads, seized supply depots, freed slaves, and pillaged or destroyed anything else that could be used to support the Confederate war machine. Though his "March to the Sea" had a military dimension, it was obvious that his campaign was also meant to terrorize the Southern populace into submission. In Atlanta, the city leaders, hearing of the atrocities committed in Sherman's wake, decided to write the general and beg that he spare the city's innocent inhabitants from such cruelty and devastation.

Atlanta, Georgia, September 11, 1864
Major-General W.T. Sherman.

Sir: We the undersigned, Mayor and two of the Council for the city of Atlanta, for the time being the only legal organ of the people of the said city, to express their wants and wishes, ask leave most earnestly but respectfully to petition you to reconsider the order requiring them to leave Atlanta.

At first view, it struck us that the measure would involve extraordinary hardship and loss, but since we have seen the practical execution of it so far as it has progressed, and the individual condition of the people, and heard their statements as to the inconveniences, loss, and suffering attending it, we are satisfied that the amount of it will involve in the aggregate consequences appalling and heart-rending.

Many poor women are in advanced state of pregnancy, others now having young children, and whose husbands for the greater part are either in the army, prisoners, or dead. Some say: "I have such a one sick at my house; who will wait on them when I am gone?" Others say: "What are we to do? We have no house to go to, and no means to buy, build, or rent any; no parents, relatives, or friends, to go to."...

We only refer to a few facts, to try to illustrate in part how this measure will operate in practice. As you advanced, the people north of this fell back; and before your arrival here, a large portion of the people had retired south, so that the country south of this is already crowded, and without houses enough to accommodate the people, and we are informed that many are now staying in churches and other out-buildings.

This being so, how is it possible for the people still here (mostly women and children) to find any shelter? And how can they live through the winter in the woods—no shelter or subsistence, in the midst of strangers who know them not, and without the power to assist them much, if they were willing to do so?

This is but a feeble picture of the consequences of this measure. You know the woe, the horrors, and the suffering, cannot be described by words; imagination can only conceive of it, and we ask you to take these things into consideration.

We know your mind and time are constantly occupied with the duties of your command, which almost deters us from asking your attention to this matter, but thought it might be that you had not considered this subject in all its awful consequences, and that on more reflection you, we hope, would not make this people an exception to all mankind, for we know of no such instance ever having occurred—surely never in the United States—and what has this helpless people done, that they should be driven from their homes, to wander strangers and outcasts, and exiles, and to subsist on charity?

We do not know as yet the number of people still here, of those who are here, we are satisfied a respectable number, if allowed to remain at home, could subsist for several months without assistance, and a respectable number for a much longer time, and who might not need assistance at any time.

In conclusion, we most earnestly and solemnly petition you to reconsider this order, or modify it, and suffer this unfortunate people to remain at home, and enjoy what little means they have.

Respectfully submitted:
James M. Calhoun, Mayor.
E.E. Rawson, Councilman.
S.C. Wells, Councilman.

Letter from the City Leaders of Atlanta to General Sherman, September 11, 1864.

General Sherman Replies to Atlanta

When he received the plea from Atlanta's civic leaders on September 11, 1864, to spare the city from destruction, General Sherman wasted little time drafting a reply. The next day he wrote out the reasons he felt compelled to carry out his original plans to eliminate any rebels around Atlanta and further deprive the Confederate army of any support that the city could provide. Sherman justifies his intentions by emphasizing his belief that

Chapter 4: The End of the Confederacy

Atop his horse, General Sherman peers through a telescope before descending on Atlanta, as civilians rush to evacuate the city.

"War is cruelty, and you cannot refine it." Furthermore, according to Sherman, the citizens of Atlanta thought nothing of supplying men and war materiel to the Southern army when it set off to harass the people of the border states, and therefore Atlanta should not be spared any wrath that might now be visited upon it.

Headquarters Military Division of the Mississippi, in the Field
Atlanta, Georgia, September 12, 1864
James M. Calhoun, Mayor, E.E. Rawson and S.C. Wells, representing City Council of Atlanta.

Gentlemen: I have your letter of the 11th, in the nature of a petition to revoke my orders removing all the inhabitants from Atlanta. I have read it carefully, and give full credit to your statements of the distress that will be occasioned, and yet shall not revoke my orders, because they were not designed to meet the humanities of the case, but to prepare for the future struggles in which millions of good people outside of Atlanta have a deep interest. We must have peace, not only at Atlanta, but in all America. To secure this, we must stop the war that now desolates our once happy and favored country. To stop war, we must defeat the rebel armies which are arrayed against the laws and Constitution that all must respect and obey. To defeat those armies, we must prepare the way to reach them in their recesses, provided with the arms and instruments which enable us to accomplish our purpose. Now, I know the vindictive nature of our enemy, that we may have many years of military operations from this quarter; and, therefore, deem it wise and prudent to prepare in time. The use of Atlanta for warlike purposes is inconsistent with its character as a home for families. There will be no manufactures, commerce, or agriculture here, for the maintenance of families, and sooner or later want will compel the inhabitants to go. Why not go now, when all the arrangements are completed for the transfer, instead of waiting till the plunging shot of contending armies will renew the scenes of the past month? Of course, I do not apprehend any such thing at this moment, but you do not suppose this army will be here until the war is over. I cannot discuss this subject with you fairly, because I cannot impart to you what we propose to do, but I assert that our military plans make it necessary for the inhabitants to go away, and I can only renew my offer of services to make their exodus in any direction as easy and comfortable as possible.

You cannot qualify war in harsher terms than I will. War is cruelty, and you cannot refine it; and those who brought war into our country deserve all the curses and maledictions a people can pour out. I know I had no hand in making this war, and I know I will make more sacrifices today than any of you to secure peace. But you cannot have peace and a division of our country. If the United States submits to a division now, it will not stop, but will go on until we reap the fate of Mexico, which is eternal war. The United States does and must assert its authority, wherever it once had power, for, if it relaxes one bit to pressure, it is gone, and I believe that such is the national feeling. This feeling assumes various shapes, but always comes back to that of Union. Once admit the Union, once more acknowledge the authority of the national Government, and, instead of devoting your houses and streets and roads to the dread uses of war, I and this army become at once your protectors and supporters, shielding you from danger, let it come from what quarter it may. I know that a few individuals cannot resist a torrent of error and passion, such as swept the South into rebellion, but you can point out, so that we may know those who desire a government, and those who insist on war and its desolation. You might as well appeal against the thunder-storm as against these terrible hardships of war. They are inevitable, and the only way the people of Atlanta can hope once more to live in peace and quiet at home, is to stop the war, which can only be done by admitting that it began in error and is perpetuated by pride. . . .

I repeat then that, by the original compact of Government, the United States had certain rights in Georgia, which have never been relinquished and never will be; that the South began war by seizing forts, arsenals, mints, custom-houses, etc., etc., long before Mr. Lincoln was installed, and before the South had one jot or tittle of provocation. I myself have seen in Missouri, Kentucky, Tennessee, and Mississippi, hundreds and thousands of women and children fleeing from your armies and desperadoes, hungry and with bleeding feet. In Memphis, Vicksburg, and Mississippi, we fed thousands upon thousands of the families of rebel soldiers left on our hands, and whom we could not see starve. Now that war comes home to you, you feel very different. You deprecate its horrors, but did not feel them when you sent carloads of soldiers and ammunition, and moulded shells and shot, to carry war into Kentucky and Tennessee, to desolate the homes of hundreds and thousands of good people who only asked to live in peace at their old homes, and under the Government of their inheritance. But these comparisons are idle. I want peace, and believe it can only be reached through union and war, and I will ever conduct war with a view to perfect and early success.

But, my dear sirs, when peace does come, you may call on me for any thing. Then will I share with you the last cracker, and watch with you to shield your homes and families against danger from every quarter.

Now you must go, and take with you the old and feeble, feed and nurse them, and build for them, in more quiet places, proper habitations to shield them against the weather until the mad passions of men cool down, and allow the Union and peace once more to settle over your old homes at Atlanta. Yours in haste,

W.T. Sherman, Major-General commanding.

Reply from General Sherman to the City Leaders of Atlanta, September 12, 1864.

The Evacuation of Richmond

Edward A. Pollard was a newspaper reporter for the Richmond Examiner *during the war. He was on hand as the Southern capital fell to Union armies under Ulysses S. Grant on April 2, 1865. Confederate commander Robert E. Lee could no longer secure Richmond and protect his right flank at Appomattox Court House, and was forced to advise city leaders to abandon the capital. Pollard reported as word reached Confederate president Jefferson Davis that he must take the government south. Pollard's account is here taken from the postwar memoirs of* New York Tribune *editor Horace Greeley, a respected Northern newsman who recognized the gift in Pollard's prose.*

While Petersburg was still held by the Confederate army, Lee saw that it could not be held much longer. His heavy losses—by this time exceeding 10,000 men—and the utter demolition of his right, rendered it morally certain that to hold on was to insure the capture or destruction of his army; and well he knew that his veterans were the last hope of the Rebellion. For Grant was now at liberty to throw forward his left to Appomattox; while it was morally certain that his cavalry would soon clutch the railroad junction at

Burkesville, which had now become the jugular vein of the gasping Confederacy. At 10:30 A.M. [April 2, 1865], therefore, he telegraphed to Davis in Richmond a dispatch, containing very nearly these words: "My lines are broken in three places. Richmond must be evacuated this evening."

That message found Mr. Davis, at 11 A.M., in church, where it was handed to him, amid an awful hush; and he immediately went quietly, soberly out—never to return as President of the Confederacy. No word was spoken; but the whole assemblage felt that the missive he had so hastily perused bore words of doom. Though the handwriting was not blazoned on the wall, it needed no Daniel to declare its import.

But no one can duly depict that last afternoon and night of Confederate rule in Richmond but an eyewitness: so let Pollard narrate for us the visible collapse and fall of the Slave Power in its chosen metropolis. After stating how, upon Mr. Davis's withdrawal from church, "the rumor was caught up in the streets that Richmond was to be evacuated, and was soon carried to the ends of the city," he proceeds:

"Men, women, and children rushed from the churches, passing from lip to lip news of the impending fall of Richmond. And yet, it was difficult to believe it. To look up to the calm, beautiful sky of that spring day, unassailed by one single noise of battle, to watch the streets, unvexed by artillery or troops, stretching away into the quiet, hazy atmosphere, and believe that the capital of the Confederacy, so peaceful, so apparently secure, was in a few hours to be the prey of the enemy, and to be wrapt in the infernal horrors of a conflagration!. . .

"Morning broke upon a scene such as those who witnessed it can never forget. The roar of an immense conflagration sounded in their ears; tongues of flame leapt from street to street; and in this baleful glare were to be seen, as of demons, the figures of busy plunderers, moving, pushing, rioting, through the black smoke and into the open street, bearing away every conceivable sort of plunder. . . ."

Jefferson Davis had left at 10 p.m. of Sunday. Nearly all the Confederate officials, including their members of Congress, had also taken their leave; as had William Smith, Governor of Virginia, and most of his satellites. There was no shadow of resistance offered to our occupation; and there is no room for doubt that a large majority of all who remained in Richmond heartily welcomed our army as deliverers.

Excerpt of the Evacuation and Fall of Richmond, by Horace Greeley and Edward A. Pollard, 1865.

Concessions at Appomattox

After Richmond fell and an assault near Petersburg failed, the remnants of the Confederate Army of Northern Virginia slipped across the Appomattox River to contemplate their dire circumstances. Hemmed in on all sides by Union forces, General Robert E. Lee finally gave the order on April 9, 1865, to open negotiations for surrender of the army to Union commander Ulysses S. Grant. The two fa-

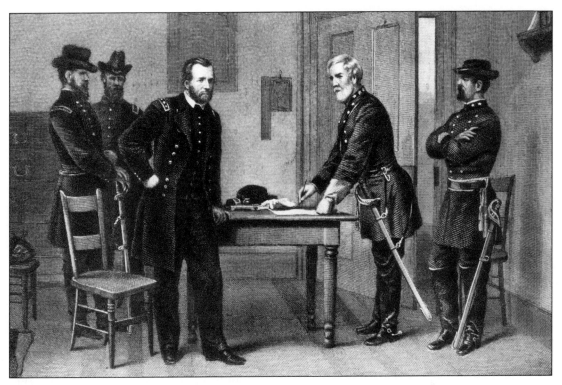

Two famous tacticians, Ulysses S. Grant (left) and Robert E. Lee, negotiate the terms of surrender at Appomattox Court House.

mous tacticians met at a farmhouse in the village of Appomattox Court House to arrange the terms. Though expecting nothing from the man known by the nickname "Unconditional Surrender," General Lee was touched by the concessions Grant was willing to make in order to bring a speedy and peaceable end to war. Union general Horace Porter was in attendance at the historic meeting, and his journal, excerpted below, records the taut yet courteous exchange between Grant and Lee.

[General Grant then began writing the terms of surrender. He wrote very rapidly, but at one point, he paused and looked at General Lee.] His eyes seemed to be resting on the handsome sword that hung at that officer's side. He said afterward that this set him to thinking that it would be an unnecessary humiliation to require the [Confederate] officers to surrender their swords, and a great hardship to deprive them of their personal baggage and horses. [As a result, Grant wrote the surrender agreement so that Confederate officers would be able to keep their horses and personal possessions. After completing the terms of surrender, Grant handed them over to Lee for him to review.]

Lee took it and laid it on the table beside him, while he drew from his pocket a pair of steel-rimmed spectacles and wiped the glasses carefully with his handkerchief. Then he crossed his legs, adjusted the spectacles very slowly and deliberately, took up the draft of the letter, and proceeded to read it attentively. It consisted of two pages.... When Lee came to the sentence about the officers' sidearms, private horses, and baggage, he showed for the first time during the reading of the letter a slight change of countenance, and was evidently touched by this act of generosity. It was doubtless the condition mentioned to which he particularly alluded when he looked toward General Grant as he finished reading and said with some degree of warmth in his manner: "This will have a very happy effect upon my army."

General Grant then said: "Unless you have some suggestions to make in regard to the form in which I have stated the terms, I will have a copy of the letter made in ink and sign it."

"There is one thing I would like to mention," Lee replied after a short pause. "The cavalrymen and artillerists own their own horses in our army. Its organization in this respect differs from that of the United States." This expression attracted the notice of our officers present, as showing how firmly the conviction was grounded in his mind that we were two distinct countries. He continued: "I would like to understand whether these men will be permitted to retain their horses?"

"You will find that the terms as written do not allow this," General Grant replied; "only the officers are permitted to take their private property."

Lee read over the second page of the letter again, and then said: "No, I see the terms do not allow it; that is clear." His face showed plainly that he was quite anxious to have this concession made, and Grant said very promptly and without giving Lee time to make a direct request:

"Well, the subject is quite new to me. Of course I did not know that any private soldiers owned their animals, but I think this will be the last battle of the war—I sincerely hope so—and that the surrender of this army will be followed soon by that of all the others, and I take it that most of the men in the [Confederate] ranks are small farmers, and as the country has been so raided by the two armies, it is doubtful whether they will be able to put in a crop to carry themselves and their families through the next winter without the aid of the horses they are now riding, and I will arrange [the surrender agreement] this way: I will not change the terms as now written, but I will instruct the officer I shall appoint to receive the paroles to let all the men who claim to own a horse or mule take the animals home with them to work their little farms."

Lee now looked greatly relieved, and though anything but a demonstrative man, he gave every evidence of his appreciation of this concession, and said, "This will have the best possible effect upon the men. It will be very gratifying and will do much toward conciliating our people."

"The Surrender at Appomattox Court House"; excerpt from *Battles and Leaders of the Civil War*, 1887.

Lee Bids Farewell to His Army

After he signed the terms of surrender, General Robert E. Lee wrote out in pencil a draft of this farewell notice to the men under his command. The short statement was then transcribed in pen by a staff officer, signed by Lee, and distributed to the troops on April 10, 1865.

Head-Quarters, Army of Northern Virginia, April 10, 1865.

After four years of arduous service, marked by unsurpassed courage and fortitude, the Army of Northern Virginia has been compelled to yield to overwhelming numbers and resources. I need not tell the survivors of so many hard-fought battles, who have remained steadfast to the last, that I have consented to this result from no distrust of them: but, feeling that valour and devotion could accomplish nothing that could compensate for the loss that would have attended the continuation of the contest, I have determined to avoid the useless sacrifice of those whose past services have endeared them to their countrymen. By the terms of the agreement, officers and men can return to their homes and remain there until exchanged. You will take with you the satisfaction that proceeds from the consciousness of duty faithfully performed; and I earnestly pray that a merciful God will extend to you His blessing and protection. With an increasing admiration of your constancy and devotion to your country, and a grateful remembrance of your kind and generous consideration of myself, I bid you an affectionate farewell.

R.E. Lee, General.

Robert E. Lee, Farewell to His Army, April 10, 1865.

"Death to All Traitors"

Even after the South's surrender, tensions between the two sides did not evaporate overnight. Many proud Southerners were unsure of how they would adjust to the collapse of their traditional way of life. The transition was not made any easier by the presence of Union armies of occupation in key Southern cities, and some rebels remained resistant to the impending changes. For Northern soldiers who had pursued the war over the course of years the end was equally fraught with high emotions. While some were eager to return home, others believed there was still work to be done. Joseph Rutherford, a surgeon with the 17th Vermont Infantry, was among the latter group. In a letter to his wife dated April 29, 1865, Rutherford expresses his belief that threats to national union will never be overcome until all those who speak of succession—both in the South and in the North—are rounded up and dealt with as traitors.

My dear Wife,

I have just received your letter of the 24th and hasten to reply to it. . . .

You ask my opinion of the affairs of the nation. What can *I* say—any more than I have often said—that we are coming out all right. The thing no doubt looks dark to you who are so far from the strife and field of battle, but to us every thing is looked upon as the fulfillment of the nations destiny. God rules our nation and the events of our terrible war. Let us bow in submision to his will, and act the part set for us to the best of our abilities.

If Sherman has done as it is said he did [negotiating lenient terms of surrender of Confederate armies in the Carolinas]—Why I think he has *dulled*—in other words made a great blunder—But so much have I become to believe in the ultimate designs of the great Ruler of all things that I feel it was intended that greater good might accrue to the nation from it. It opens the eyes of the people to the gross folly of being too lenient to these hell born traitors not only at the South but in the midst of our N.E. [New England] homes. We are all coming home soon: and our first work will be to clean out every traitor and tory [opponent of the Republican party]—that act as foul ulcers in the living flesh of our homes. We soldiers have *vowed* it upon the alter [*sic*] of our country and you may depend the poisonous blood of these treacherous villians will flow freely, for the lives of many of our noble soldiers they have been the means of sacrificing. God have mercy on them for we wont—*No! Never.* . . .

You may think me excited and so I am but it is an excitement that nothing but the just punishment of traitors will allay. The country will never be safe while they are allowed to walk its surface or breathe the air of heaven—Death to all traitors is our watch word.

Joseph C. Rutherford, letter to Hannah Rutherford, April 29, 1865.

The Death of Abraham Lincoln

On April 14, only five days after Robert E. Lee surrendered at Appomattox, President Abraham Lincoln was mortally wounded by Southern loyalists at Ford's Theatre in Washington D.C. His body was conveyed immediately to a nearby boardinghouse where government officials as well as Lincoln's wife and son, Robert, kept vigil through the night. Gideon Welles, Lincoln's secretary of the navy, was one of those who rushed to the president's side. In his diary, Welles recorded what transpired in the boardinghouse over the several hours it took for Lincoln to finally expire from his wound.

As we descended the stairs, I asked [Secretary of War Edwin] Stanton what he had heard in regard to the President that was reliable. He said the President was shot at Ford's Theatre, that he had seen a man who was present and witnessed the occurrence. I said I would go immediately to the White House. Stanton told me the President was not there but was at the theatre. "Then," said I, "let us go immediately there."

The President had been carried across the street from the theatre, to the house of a Mr. Peterson. We entered by ascending a flight of steps above the basement and passing through a long hall to the rear, where the President lay extended on a bed, breathing heavily. Several surgeons were present, at least six, I should think more. Among them I was glad to observe Dr. Hall, who, however, soon left. I inquired of Dr. H., as I entered, the true condition of the President. He replied the President was dead to all intents, although he might live three hours or perhaps longer.

The giant sufferer lay extended diagonally across the bed, which was not long enough for him. He had been stripped of his clothes. His large arms, which were occasionally exposed, were of a size which one would scarce have expected from his spare appearance. His slow, full respiration lifted the clothes with each breath that he took. His features were calm and striking. I had never seen them appear to better advantage than for the first hour, perhaps, that I was there. After that, his right eye began to swell and that part of his face became discolored.

Senator [Charles] Sumner was there, I think, when I entered. If not he came in soon after, as did Speaker [of the House Schuyler] Colfax, Mr. Secretary [of the Treasury Hugh] McCulloch, and the other members of the Cabinet, with the exception of Mr. Seward. A double guard was stationed at the door and on the sidewalk, to repress the crowd, which was of course highly excited and anxious. The room was small and overcrowded. The surgeons and members of the Cabinet were as many as should have been in the room, but there

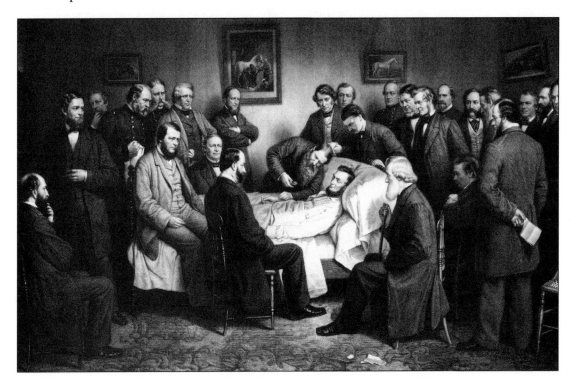

Government officials surround President Lincoln, who was mortally wounded by John Wilkes Booth at Ford's Theatre.

were many more, and the hall and other rooms in the front or main house were full. One of these rooms was occupied by Mrs. Lincoln and her attendants, with Miss Harris. Mr. Dixon and Mrs. Kinney came to her about twelve o'clock. About once an hour Mrs. Lincoln would repair to the bedside of her dying husband and with lamentation and tears remain until overcome by emotion.

A little before seven, I went into the room where the dying President was rapidly drawing near the closing moments. His wife soon after made her last visit to him. The death-struggle had begun. Robert, his son, stood with several others at the head of the bed. He bore himself well, but on two occasions gave way to overpowering grief and sobbed aloud, turning his head and leaning on the shoulder of Senator Sumner. The respiration of the President became suspended at intervals, and at last entirely ceased at twenty-two minutes past seven. . . .

I went after breakfast to the Executive Mansion. There was a cheerless cold rain and everything seemed gloomy. On the Avenue in front of the White House were several hundred colored people, mostly women and children, weeping and wailing their loss. This crowd did not appear to diminish through the whole of that cold, wet day; they seemed not to know what was to be their fate since their great benefactor was dead, and their hopeless grief affected me more than almost anything else, though strong and brave men wept when I met them.

Gideon Welles, *Diary of Gideon Welles*, 1911.

★ Chronology of Events ★

1820
The Missouri Compromise allows Maine into the Union as a free state and Missouri as a slave state. Slavery is also to be banned from new territories above 36' 30' longitude (except Missouri).

1850
Senator Henry Clay pushes legislation that will be called the Compromise of 1850. Its provisions allow California into the Union as a free state, while the territories of Utah and New Mexico are to determine by popular vote whether they will allow slavery in their borders. The South is to be appeased by the passing of a tougher Fugitive Slave Act, requiring that escaped slaves caught in Northern states be returned to their owners.

June 16, 1858
Senatorial candidate Abraham Lincoln of Illinois delivers his "A House Divided" speech which declares that no nation can long exist half free and half slave. Lincoln loses his bid for Congress.

November 4, 1860
Running on the Republican ticket, Lincoln wins the presidential election.

December 20, 1860
South Carolina becomes the first state to secede from the Union. Within a month, six other Southern states will join it.

February 18, 1861
Jefferson Davis is inaugurated as the president of the Confederate States of America.

March 4, 1861
Lincoln is inaugurated as the sixteenth president of the United States.

April 12, 1861
Confederate guns fire on Fort Sumter. Federal commander Major Robert Anderson surrenders the fort two days later.

July 21, 1861
Confederate troops win a victory at the First Battle of Bull Run in Manassas, Virginia.

February 6–16, 1862
General Ulysses S. Grant captures Forts Henry and Donelson in Tennessee.

April 6–7, 1862
Grant's army is surprised at the Battle of Shiloh in Tennessee. After two days of fighting Grant pushes back the Confederate attack. More soldiers die in the two days than have been killed in all previous U.S. wars combined.

May 31–June 1, 1862
At the Battle of Fair Oaks, bad luck and poor communication hamper the Confederate forces and the two sides fight to a draw. As a result, Jefferson Davis removes Joseph E. Johnston from command of the Army of

Northern Virginia and replaces him with Robert E. Lee.

September 17, 1862
Battle of Antietam (Sharpsburg) witnesses the bloodiest day of the war as more than twenty-five thousand men become casualties.

September 22, 1862
Lincoln issues the Emancipation Proclamation, which is to take effect on January 1, 1863. The proclamation frees all slaves in territories rebelling against the Union.

March 3, 1863
Congress passes the Enrollment Act of 1863, effectively instituting a draft. Riots against conscription arise in several Northern cities, most notably New York.

July 1–3, 1863
Union general George Meade and Confederate general Robert E. Lee clash at Gettysburg, Pennsylvania. After a disastrous charge on the third day of fighting, Lee is forced to withdraw, ending his invasion of the North.

November 19, 1863
Lincoln attends a dedication of the military cemetery at Gettysburg. There, he reads a short speech honoring those who fight in the name of the nation's ideals. His words became known as the Gettysburg Address.

November–December, 1864
General William T. Sherman marches his Union army across Georgia, destroying Confederate supplies and reducing rebel morale.

January 31, 1865
Congress approves the Thirteenth Amendment to the Constitution to abolish slavery in America.

March 14, 1865
Jefferson Davis's government passes a measure that authorizes the use of freed blacks and slaves in military service.

April 2, 1865
Union troops march unopposed into the Confederate capital at Richmond.

April 9, 1865
Lee surrenders to Grant at Appomattox Court House.

April 14, 1865
Lincoln is assassinated by John Wilkes Booth, a Confederate sympathizer.

December 13, 1865
The Thirteenth Amendment is ratified by the states.

★ Index ★

abolition, 7
  economic reasons for, 12
  Women's National Loyal League and, 59
  see also Emancipation Proclamation
African Americans
  in Confederate army, 68–69
  free Southern, 68–69
  in Union army
    Copperheads and, 60–61
    Emancipation Proclamation and, 47
    54th Massachusetts Regiment, 52
    19th Colored Infantry, 53
    treatment of, 57–59
  see also slavery
agriculture, 7
Alexander, Edward Porter, 38–39
Anderson, Robert, 29
Anthony, Susan B., 59–60
Antietam, Battle of, 53–55
Appomattox Courthouse (Virginia), 71, 83
Army of Northern Virginia, 71, 82–84, 85
Army of the Potomac, 29
Atlanta, Georgia, 77–81

battles. *See names of individual battles*

Blackwood's Edinburgh Magazine, 39–41
Border States, 26–27
Brewster, Charles Harvey, 41–42
Britain, 47–48
Buchanan, James, 18–20
Buckner, S.B., 71–72
Bull Run, Battle of, 36–39
Burnside, Ambrose, 45–46

Calhoun, James M., 78
Calhoun, John C., 10–11
California, 7
Chambersburg, Pennsylvania, 65
Chesnut, Mary Boykin, 29–31
Chicago Times (newspaper), 26–27
Chicago Tribune (newspaper), 71–72, 73
Chickasaw (Union ship), 77
Choctaw, 63–64
Civil War
  belief that it would be brief, 28, 31, 34, 73
  effects on civilians, 31–32, 79, 80–81
  Emancipation Proclamation and purpose of, 47

  as necessary, 21–23
  as unnecessary, 13–14, 18
Clay, Henry, 8–9
Colfax, Schuyler, 86
Compromise of 1850
  balance of power in Congress and, 7–8, 9–10
  Southern reaction to, 8, 9–11
Confederacy, the
  army of
    African Americans in, 68–69
    Army of Northern Virginia, 71, 82–84, 85
    soldiers of
      described, 39–41
      morale of, 67–68
      recruitment of, 33–34
      shortage of, 71, 74
      uniforms for, 48–49
    strategy of, 28, 38
    surrender of, 71, 82–84, 85, 86
  blockade of, 71
  Choctaw and, 63–64
  Europe and, 47–48
  fall of Richmond and, 81–82
  see also South, the
Congress, balance of power in

Compromise of 1850 and, 7–8, 9–10
Missouri Compromise and, 7
secession and, 13
Senate, 8
Constitution
  conscription of soldiers and, 62–63
  permanent nature of, 9, 25–26
  property rights in, 19, 20
  slavery in, 15
  states' rights in, 10–11
Cooke, John Esten, 42–44
Copperheads, 60–61
Cormany, Rachel, 65
cotton, 48

Davis, Jefferson
  Battle of Bull Run and, 38, 39
  fall of Richmond and, 82
  inaugural address of, 23–24
  on secession, 23–24
De Bow's Review (journal), 13–14
Declaration of Independence, 24
Democratic Party, 8
Douglas, Stephen, 15
draft riots, 61–63

economy
  of the North, 7–8
  of the South, 7, 11–12
Emancipation Proclamation
  abolitionists and, 59

effect of, on the South, 47–48, 67–68
Europe and, 47–48
issuance of, 47
provisions of, 47, 55–57
Union army and, 47
Enrollment Act, 61
Europe, 47–48

Fair Oaks, Battle of, 41–42
Farragut, David, 75–77
54th Massachusetts Regiment, 52
Ford's Theatre, 86
Fort Donelson, 70, 71
Fort Henry, 70, 71
Fort Moultrie, 22
Fort Sumter, 26, 28, 29–31
France, 48
Fredericksburg, Battle of, 45–46
Fugitive Slave Act, 7

Georgia, 71, 77–81
Gettysburg, Battle of, 65
Gettysburg Address, 66–67
Gooding, James Henry, 57–59
Grant, Ulysses S.
  Lincoln and, 70, 71
  reputation of, 70, 71–72, 74
  Richmond and, 81–82
  strategy of, 71, 73, 74
  surrender and Lee's, 82–84
  unconditional, 71–72
Greeley, Horace
  on fall of Richmond, 81–82

on secession, 17–18

Hammond, James Henry, 16–17
Hartford (Union ship), 75, 77
Helper, Hinton R., 11–12
Holsinger, Frank, 53–55
Horton, George, 54
"House Divided, A," 15–16

Impending Crisis of the South: How to Meet It, The (Helper), 11–12
Indianapolis Daily Journal (newspaper), 21–23
industrialization, 7, 28

Jackson, Stonewall, 38

Kansas-Nebraska Act, 15
Kansas Territory, 19

Lackawanna (Union ship), 76, 77
Lee, Robert E.
  fall of Richmond and, 81–82
  farewell to Army of Northern Virginia, 85
  strategy of, 65, 70–71
  surrender of, 71, 82–84
"Lee's Hill," 45
Lincoln, Abraham
  "A House Divided," 15–16
  as commander-in-chief
    Burnside and, 45
    Grant and, 70, 71
    McClellan and, 45
  pardons by, 53

INDEX

soldiers and, 32–33
death of, 86–88
election of, as president, 20–21
Emancipation Proclamation, 47, 48, 55–57, 67–68
first inaugural address of, 24–26
Gettysburg Address, 66–67
on secession, 24–26
Senate race of, 8, 14–16

Maine, 7
Manassas, Battle of, 28, 36–39
Manhattan (Union ship), 77
"March to the Sea," 77
Martin, William T., 43
McClellan, George B., 29, 41, 45
McCulloch, Hugh, 86
McDowell, Irvin, 36
Meade, George, 54, 65
Missouri Compromise, 7, 15
Mobile, Alabama, 75–77
Monongahela (Union ship), 76
morale
 in the North
  of civilians, 34–35
  after death of Lincoln, 86
  of soldiers, 53
 in the South
  of civilians, 30–31, 48–49

of soldiers, 67–68
Morgan, Sarah, 50–52
Myers, A.C., 33–34

Nebraska doctrine, 15
neutrality, 26–27
New York City draft riots, 61–63
New York Times (newspaper), 34–36
New York Tribune (newspaper), 17–18
19th Colored Infantry, 53
North, the
 economy of, 7–8
 invasion of, 65
 political power of, 11
 women of, 59, 60
 working-class white slaves in, 16, 17
 see also Union, the

Patterson, Edmund DeWitt, 67–68
Pitchlynn, P.P., 63–64
Pollard, Edward A., 81, 82
Porter, Horace, 83–84
property rights, 19, 20

Rawson, E.E., 78
Republican Party, 8
Rhodes, Elisha Hunt, 46
Richmond, Virginia
 evacuation of, 81–82
 protection of, 28, 29
Richmond Examiner (newspaper), 81, 82
Ruffin, Edmund, 13–14
Russell, William, 31, 37–38
Rutherford, Joseph, 85–86

secession
 causes of, 20–21
 Clay on, 8–9
 Davis on, 23–24
 Greeley on, 17–18
 Lincoln on, 24–26
 reasons for, 23–24
 right to, 18, 21–23
 Ruffin on, 13–14
 of South Carolina, 8, 20–21
 treatment of supporters of, after Civil War, 86
 war as response to, 13–14, 18, 21–23
Sharpsburg, Battle of, 47
Shaw, Robert Gould, 52–53
Sherman, William T., 71, 77–81
69th Regiment of New York, 34–36
slavery
 army of the Confederacy and, 69
 in Constitution, 15
 Copperheads and, 60–61
 extension of, 7, 15–16, 19
 justification of, 16–17
 as obstacle to growth of the South's economy, 11–12
 Republican Party and, 8
 of working-class white slaves in the North, 16, 17
 see also abolition; Emancipation Proclamation
Smith, William, 82
South, the
 economy of, 7, 11–12

effect of Emancipation Proclamation on, 47–48, 67–68
free African Americans in, 68–69
nonslaveholding whites of, 12
political power of the North and, 11
reaction to Compromise of 1850 in, 8, 9–11
women in
behavior of, 50–52
living conditions in Atlanta, 77–78
war effort of, 48–49
see also Confederacy, the
South Carolina, 8, 20–21
Spotsylvania Court House, Battle of, 74–75
Stanton, Edwin, 86
Stanton, Elizabeth Cady, 59–60
state militias, 32–33
states' rights, 10–11, 20
Stephens, George E., 60–61
Stiles, Robert, 45–46
Stuart, J.E.B. (Jeb), 42–44
Sumner, Charles, 86

Tecumseh (Union ship), 75
Tennessee (Confederate ship), 75–77
territories, slavery in, 7, 15–16, 19

Union, the
army of
Army of the Potomac, 29
Emancipation Proclamation and, 47
government in affairs of, 52–53
McClellan and, 29
69th Regiment of New York, 34–36
soldiers of, 46
conscription of, 61–63
equipment of, 34
morale of, 53
number of, 71
state militias and, 32–33
volunteer, 31–32
strategy of, 71
navy of, 75–77
see also, African Americans, in Union army; North, the
Upson, Theodore, 31–32

Watson, J. Crittenden, 75
Wearing of the Gray (Cooke), 42–44
Weekly Anglo-African (journal), 60–61
Wells, Gideon, 86–88
Wells, S.C., 78
women
in the North, 59, 60
in the South
behavior of, 50–52
living conditions in Atlanta, 77–78
war effort of, 48–49
Women's National Loyal League, 59

★ Picture Credits ★

Cover Photo, Library of Congress
© Bettmann/CORBIS, 59, 62, 76, 79
© CORBIS, 40
Hulton/Archive by Getty Images, 9, 10, 23, 43, 66, 74, 83
Library of Congress, 14, 25, 30, 35, 36, 44, 58, 72, 87
North Wind Picture Archive, 56
© Richard T. Nowitz/CORBIS

★ About the Editor ★

Author David M. Haugen edits books for Lucent Books and Greenhaven Press. He holds a master's degree in English literature and has also worked as a writer and instructor.